MEGA

Mild/Moderate Cross Categorical Special Education (050)

SECRETS

Study Guide
Your Key to Exam Success

MEGA Test Review for the
Missouri Educator Gateway Assessments

Dear Future Exam Success Story:

Congratulations on your purchase of our study guide. Our goal in writing our study guide was to cover the content on the test, as well as provide insight into typical test taking mistakes and how to overcome them.

Standardized tests are a key component of being successful, which only increases the importance of doing well in the high-pressure high-stakes environment of test day. How well you do on this test will have a significant impact on your future, and we have the research and practical advice to help you execute on test day.

The product you're reading now is designed to exploit weaknesses in the test itself, and help you avoid the most common errors test takers frequently make.

How to use this study guide

We don't want to waste your time. Our study guide is fast-paced and fluff-free. We suggest going through it a number of times, as repetition is an important part of learning new information and concepts.

First, read through the study guide completely to get a feel for the content and organization. Read the general success strategies first, and then proceed to the content sections. Each tip has been carefully selected for its effectiveness.

Second, read through the study guide again, and take notes in the margins and highlight those sections where you may have a particular weakness.

Finally, bring the manual with you on test day and study it before the exam begins.

Your success is our success

We would be delighted to hear about your success. Send us an email and tell us your story. Thanks for your business and we wish you continued success.

Sincerely,

Mometrix Test Preparation Team

Need more help? Check out our flashcards at: http://MometrixFlashcards.com/MEGA

TABLE OF CONTENTS

Top 20 Test Taking Tips

1. Carefully follow all the test registration procedures
2. Know the test directions, duration, topics, question types, how many questions
3. Setup a flexible study schedule at least 3-4 weeks before test day
4. Study during the time of day you are most alert, relaxed, and stress free
5. Maximize your learning style; visual learner use visual study aids, auditory learner use auditory study aids
6. Focus on your weakest knowledge base
7. Find a study partner to review with and help clarify questions
8. Practice, practice, practice
9. Get a good night's sleep; don't try to cram the night before the test
10. Eat a well balanced meal
11. Know the exact physical location of the testing site; drive the route to the site prior to test day
12. Bring a set of ear plugs; the testing center could be noisy
13. Wear comfortable, loose fitting, layered clothing to the testing center; prepare for it to be either cold or hot during the test
14. Bring at least 2 current forms of ID to the testing center
15. Arrive to the test early; be prepared to wait and be patient
16. Eliminate the obviously wrong answer choices, then guess the first remaining choice
17. Pace yourself; don't rush, but keep working and move on if you get stuck
18. Maintain a positive attitude even if the test is going poorly
19. Keep your first answer unless you are positive it is wrong
20. Check your work, don't make a careless mistake

Students with Mild to Moderate Disabilities

Piaget's stages of cognitive development

Sensorimotor stage

Piaget defined four stages of cognitive development. He called the first stage sensorimotor to characterize infants' cognitive processes: they perceive sensory information from their surrounding environments and respond to these by engaging in motor activities, e.g., rooting, suckling, looking, listening, reaching, and grasping. Piaget divided the sensorimotor stage into six substages: Reflexes, from 0–1 month; Primary Circular Reactions from 1–4 months wherein infants finds accidental actions like thumb-sucking pleasurable and then intentionally repeats them; Secondary Circular Reactions from 4–8 months when infants intentionally repeat actions to evoke environmental effects; Coordination of Reactions from 8–12 months, featuring obviously intentional actions, comprehension of cause and effect, and combining schemas (concepts); Tertiary Circular Reactions from 12–18 months, when children experiment with trial-and-error; and Early Representational Thought from 18–24 months, when children begin representing things or events with symbols. A significant sensorimotor development is Object Permanence, i.e., realizing things still exist when out of sight.

Preoperational stage

Piaget called his second stage of cognitive development, between the ages of 2–7 years, Preoperational, because children have not yet developed the ability to perform mental operations, i.e., mentally manipulating information, and do not understand concrete logic. Piaget called children in this stage egocentric, i.e., they cannot assume another's perspective. For example, Preoperational children can select a picture matching a three-dimensional scene they just saw, but cannot select a picture matching what someone else would see from a different physical location/position. They do not understand what Piaget termed conservation, the concept that quantities remain constant regardless of shape or appearance. For example, children judge the same amount of liquid differently by its appearance in differently shaped containers (short wide versus tall narrow), even when seeing it poured from one to the other. Piaget identified additional characteristics of Preoperational thinking as animism (attributing human qualities to inanimate objects) and magical thinking (attributing external events to one's internal thoughts).

Concrete Operations stage

Around ages 7–11 years, children are in what Piaget termed the Concrete Operations stage. A salient feature of this stage is that children develop the ability to think logically and conduct mental operations with regard to concrete objects. However, they still have trouble comprehending hypothetical and abstract concepts. A significant ability developing during this stage is the understanding of reversibility, i.e., that actions can be reversed. Whereas the younger Preoperational child watching someone pour liquid from a short, wide container to a tall, narrow one believes the taller container has more liquid, the Concrete Operations child sees the amount is the same despite different container shapes. Reversibility aids this insight. Children in Concrete Operations also understand sequences between mental categories, e.g., their pet is a poodle, a poodle is a dog, and a dog is an animal. The introduction of formal school subjects, especially math, is no coincidence with the age range of this stage because children in Concrete Operations are first able to do simple arithmetic computations.

<u>Formal Operations</u>

Piaget termed his final stage of cognitive development, from around age 12 into adulthood, as Formal Operations. This reflects the individual's ability to understand and manipulate completely abstract concepts without needing to refer to concrete objects. This stage also features the development of logic, the addition of deductive reasoning to the inductive reasoning children develop in the previous stage of Concrete Operations, and systematic planning. Children/teens/adults can now consider hypothetical situations; apply general principles to predict specific events (deductive reasoning) as well as make generalizations from multiple specific details (inductive reasoning, which typically develops during Concrete Operations); and plan organized, systematic approaches to problem-solving. They are more fully able to consider another's viewpoint and feelings, and can understand abstract concepts like liberty, justice, democracy, truth, and beauty.

Delays in cognitive development

Whether caused by neurological deficits or damage, deprivation or other environmental factors, or a combination, some children do not develop cognitive skills typically. They may develop them much later than others or not at all. They may also demonstrate differences in the quantity and quality of their cognitive skills. Children with cognitive developmental delays, for example, can have significant difficulty with learning colors, shapes, and similar basic concepts. They often have trouble learning more advanced concepts, such as counting numbers, reading printed language, and writing language. In addition, children with delayed and/or deficient cognitive development can demonstrate a failure to generalize things they learn to other situations or contexts. Moreover, when children have problems with adjusting to new situations and changes in their environments, this can be a sign of delayed or deficient cognitive development.

Atypical social and emotional development

When children experience developmental delays that are manifested in the social and emotional domain, one characteristic is being too trusting of others, which allows others to take advantage of them. This is often associated with intellectual disability or intellectual disabilities. Another characteristic of some children with atypical social and emotional development is not reading or understanding others' nonverbal cues indicating emotional states or social conventions, and/or linguistic cues during interpersonal interactions, preventing them from responding appropriately. This is commonly associated with autism spectrum disorders. Autistic children also may show excellent verbal skills in monologues, but be unable to initiate and maintain conversations and have difficulty with turn-taking. Some children fail to develop the ability to consider others' viewpoints at typical ages, remaining egocentric; this interferes with social interaction. This is common to various conditions, including intellectual disability, autism, and behavior disorders. Children with ADHD tend to have difficulties with impulse control, emotional self-regulation, and sustaining attention, interfering with social interactions as much as with academic performance.

Atypical development of gross motor skills

Motor development follows a hierarchical pattern. In other words, for example, if a child cannot stand, s/he cannot walk, and if s/he cannot walk, s/he cannot run. When a baby is between 3 and 12 months old, some signs of atypical gross motor skills development include that the child does not open his/her hands during the normal age range; that the child has trouble holding his/her head up; the child cannot sit up without support, and/or the child has difficulty sitting up even with support; and the child does not begin to pull up on furniture or stand up during this age range. Between 12 and 36 months, signs of delayed/atypical development include problems with walking and/or running; with ascending or descending stairs; with rolling, catching, and throwing a ball; and with jumping and hopping. Children with atypical motor development may demonstrate higher or lower muscle tone than normal and problems with motor planning, motor coordination, balance, and proprioception.

Fine motor skills

Young children need fine motor skills to play with toys, eat meals, turn lights on/off, and hold crayons, paintbrushes, spoons, etc. During evaluations, many children perform poorly on certain tasks, from delays not in cognitive development but in fine motor development. Oral/motor skills, like the control of jaw, lip, mouth, and tongue movements for eating and speaking, are included in fine motor skills. While occupational therapists work with other fine motor skills, speech-language pathologists and occupational therapists may both work to remediate oral/motor skill deficits. If a baby has trouble orally grasping the nipple or bottle to nurse, this can indicate delayed fine motor development. Babies whose hands are in fists more often than open may have fine motor delays. A baby having problems manually bringing toys to his/her mouth and/or mouthing them can have atypical fine motor development. Difficulty holding small objects with a pincer grasp or with a thumb and a forefinger is another sign of delayed fine motor development.

Early language development

The development of language skills is critical to the development of cognitive, emotional, and social skills. These are all interrelated, so problems in any one area usually cause problems/delays in others. Receptive language is the ability to understand spoken and written language. Receptive language develops before expressive language: children must understand what they hear before they learn to speak, and to read and comprehend written language before they learn to write. Hence a child's receptive vocabulary typically exceeds his/her expressive vocabulary: s/he can understand more words than s/he can use. Nonverbal receptive language includes understanding others' facial expressions. Verbal receptive language includes understanding what others say; understanding qualitative concepts like big/little and tall/short and quantitative concepts like a lot, a little, all, none, etc.; understanding and following simple directions; listening to stories; understanding and following complex/multiple directions to do a series of things; and understanding others' questions. Written receptive language includes identifying upper- and lowercase letters and numbers, and also reading and comprehending simple and complex sentences and paragraphs.

Receptive, expressive, and pragmatic language and delayed or atypical development

Receptive language is comprehending language we hear and read. Expressive language is our production of spoken and written language. Pragmatic language is our using receptive and expressive language to facilitate social interactions. Expressive and pragmatic language depend upon receptive language, which precedes them. If a baby is not imitating others' vocal sounds or behaviors or responding to hearing his/her name called and/or seems not to be listening to others' speech by the age of 12 months, this can indicate delayed/deficient receptive language development. By three years, if a child does not follow instructions and/or does not learn to speak normally, this can indicate receptive language delay. When children frequently ask others to repeat and/or have trouble answering questions by five years old, they may have receptive language delays. By seven years, signs of receptive language deficits include having trouble understanding stories told/read aloud; avoiding participating in social activities; and having trouble processing or making sense of verbal information. Having trouble reading sentences by nine years old is another sign.

Expressive language development

Expressive language is that language we produce in order to communicate with others, whether through spoken or written words, vocal sounds, facial expressions, physical gestures, and/or body language. Babies and children develop expressive language gradually and in a cumulative sequence. Nonverbal expressive language consists of all of that expressive communication that does not involve the use of words. For example, when a baby cries, that is a form of nonverbal expressive language. Smiling also communicates pleasure, recognition, and/or affection toward others. Laughing expresses amusement or delight. Frowning expresses displeasure, sadness, or anger. When infants and toddlers learn to wave "bye-bye," they are using nonverbal expressive language. When babies and young children point at things, they nonverbally communicate a variety of messages—like "I want that"; "Look at that"; "What is that?"; "I see that." When young children throw objects, whether to express anger, protest something, or get an adult to retrieve it as a game, this is also nonverbal expressive language.

Vocal and spoken verbal expressive language in babies and young children: Verbal expressive language can be spoken or written. In infants, early forms of verbalization also include vocalizations. For example, babies "coo" by repeating prolonged vowel sounds; "grunt" or make guttural sounds expressing satisfaction/contentedness; and soon begin to babble by repeating consonant-vowel combinations like "bababababa," "dadadada," etc. Babies also imitate adults' vocal sounds and facial expressions. Their first words are often parent names like "Mama" and "Dada," which coincide closely with babbling sounds. As their speech develops, they echo/repeat others' utterances. In the holophrastic stage, toddlers use single words to express phrase concepts, like "up" to mean "Pick me up" or "Look at the bird up there." They combine pointing with nouns to identify people, animals, and things, like "baby," "doggie," or "car." They soon learn to use the socially conventional utterances "thank you" and "please." Toddlers then learn to combine two words to express phrase concepts, like "Daddy go" or "Mommy shoe," which can also convey a variety of meanings.

Development of spoken verbal expressive language skills: Once they can speak using more than one-word expressions, young children begin to ask questions and answer others' questions. They progress to correctly using words expressing qualitative concepts, including opposites like big and little, tall and short, etc.; and quantitative concepts, including opposite and relative quantities like all, none, a lot, or a little. As their expressive language skills develop, they reflect children's receptive understanding of the concepts underlying the words. The toddler's basic "She walk" phrase gives way to the more advanced present progressive verb tense "She is walking" in preschoolers. Children begin to use pronouns like "I" and "you," rather than using no pronouns or only "me" or "Mommy." They then develop possessive pronouns like "mine" and "my" [+ object]. They start including prepositions like on, in, over, and under. They use past tenses, both regular and irregular ("gave") and future constructions like "will/is going to" [+verb]. They progress from two-word to three- and four-word phrases, and then full sentences with subject, auxiliary verb, verb, and object.

Activities that reflect written expressive language skills development: Children learn to speak before they learn to write, though there is also some overlap in their developing spoken and written expressive language skills. These both also depend on the development of the receptive language skills of listening and reading comprehension. Young children first learn to trace letters, then they copy them, and then they write them. They follow the same progression with tracing, copying, and writing numbers. They copy examples of simple words, like "Mom," and then do the same with more complex words like "truck." Once they have copied words and can remember letters, they progress to writing the letters in sequence to spell written words (d-a-d-d-y). Thereafter, they learn to write consecutive words that form sentences, such as "I love my kitty." Eventually, school-age children can write connected sentences that form paragraphs, like "I love my kitty. One day my friends will come over. I will show my kitty to my friends."

Signs in babies and young children are of atypical development or delays: Babies normally babble at a few to several months. An infant's not babbling by eight months is a sign of delayed/atypical spoken language development. A child not uttering any words by 18 months is not developing expressive language normally. Children over two years using only single words show atypical development. After four years, speaking mainly in "baby talk" is atypical. Echolalia (continually repeating what others say) is normal in younger children, but beyond three years is atypical. Talking to oneself aloud is typical of toddlers, but children continuing this practice extensively past three years show delayed development. Children older than three years who do not take conversational turns but talk "in circles" are not developing typically. Children over four years who have trouble expressing their needs and wants show atypical development. Answering open-ended questions ("What did you do at Jimmy's?") with single words indicates a delay in a six-year-old. Overgeneralizing, i.e., naming many objects with one word like calling all vehicles cars, is another sign of delayed expressive language development.

Babies who make no, or very little, eye contact with others by 12 months of age are not developing typically. Another sign indicating a need for evaluation is not pointing at things by this age. Children who demonstrate few or no skills at taking turns by a year old can have expressive language delays. Little or no demonstration of joint attention, i.e., attending to the same thing as his/her parent, is another sign of developmental delay. So is a lack of joint action, i.e., engaging in the same activity as the parent. Children who consistently hit others or have temper tantrums when they cannot communicate a message to others show signs of delayed expressive language. Crying, yelling, and similar shows of frustration when trying to communicate also indicate developmental delays. In addition, young children with such delays may rarely if ever initiate conversations with others, and may not want to engage in activities with others.

Physical and motor development of children with Down syndrome

Children with Down syndrome show overall slower development in physiology and motor skills. They grow more slowly in physical size and also ultimately attain smaller full statures than typically developing children. They tend to have lower/weaker muscle tone, or hypotonia. They commonly start walking significantly later than other children. Even once they learn to walk, they may not develop physical coordination, balance, and proprioception as soon or ever as well as other children. The oral-motor skills components of motor development are also slower to develop in those with Down syndrome, compounded by having large, thick, often protruding tongues, which can interfere with eating skills and clear speech. Additional physiological stigmata of Down syndrome include small hands and feet; short, stubby fingers; short, thick necks; small heads, flattened in back; small noses; and Asian-appearing eyes with epicanthal folds. Down syndrome children are more likely to have celiac disease (gluten intolerance), gastroesophageal reflux, hypothyroidism, hearing and vision problems, and to develop senile dementias earlier than normally.

Development of students with autism spectrum disorders

<u>Language</u>
An estimated one-half of those on the autism spectrum never develop verbal language skills. The other half range from echolalia as their only speech production to perfectly functional, high-level speech, and everything in between. Some autistic students display advanced vocabularies and fluent speech in long monologues about topics interesting them, often including the highly specialized and/or technical, but are unable to initiate or maintain two-way conversations with others. These individuals have difficulty with turn-taking and the give-and-take of verbal interactions. Some high-functioning autistic persons can conduct normal conversations with others, but their speech patterns may sound a bit singsong, odd, or quirky. Many autistic students have difficulty understanding emotional overtones in others' speech, such as sarcasm or humor. Additionally, they often cannot understand nonverbal cues like facial expressions, gestures, and body language indicating emotions or social customs, though many can learn this through explicit training.

<u>Social and emotional</u>
Emotional and social differences can be observed in autistic people from early childhood, when many of them avoid eye contact with others and resist physical contact with parents, like flinging themselves backward from being hugged/held or going rigid in their bodies when held. Many also engage in repetitive, stereotypic self-stimulating behaviors like rocking. Students with autism experience the same internal emotions as others, but may not express these normally. Moreover, they often have great difficulty noticing or understanding the emotions of others and their expression of them. As a result, their behavior in social situations can appear rather strange, especially from high-functioning autistic individuals with above-average intelligence. For example, as autism expert John Gerdtz once related, "It's really strange when you're talking with someone who has a PhD in mathematics, and he suddenly turns and walks away right in the middle of the conversation." Autistic individuals frequently fail to follow social conventions because they do not understand them.

<u>Behavioral differences</u>
One area of behavioral difference among the autistic is language: some people with autism spectrum disorders (ASDs) have few or no verbal skills; others have limited speech and

- 7 -

language; others have more functional, but odd-sounding speech and language; and still others have highly functioning verbal skills. Some are able to speak extensively on favorite topics but cannot start or continue social conversations. Another area is social and emotional: those with ASDs have difficulty observing, interpreting, and using socially accepted behaviors indicating emotions. A common autistic deficit is tolerating interruptions, changes, or transitions in activities. Autistic people frequently display narrowly limited interests and activities, and rigid thinking and behavior. The lower functioning often engage in repetitive behaviors; the higher functioning can focus intensely on a single activity for long periods, but not shift or divide their attention. Some autistic individuals react to sudden changes, or sensory input they find painful due to hypersensitivity, with panic reactions including screaming, self-injurious behavior, and/or withdrawal into rocking, counting, or other repetitive self-soothing actions.

Deaf students

Differences in learning
Hearing children are surrounded by speech sounds from birth, and they absorb a great deal of their knowledge and understanding of language and speech through this immersion. However, deaf children do not benefit from sensory input in the auditory mode. Those whose parents use sign language and/or speech reading learn to comprehend and produce language through the visual modality instead. This is a major difference, because the main basis for communication among the majority of the population is auditory; and written language, with its relationship to spoken language, has the same auditory basis. Instead of auditory cues like tone of voice, grammatical inflections (like verb tense or plural endings), or intonations like the rising end of a question, deaf students rely exclusively on visual cues like facial expressions, gestures, and body language; and in ASL (American Sign Language), built-in signs conveying grammatical information.

Similarities to hearing students
Although a major difference in deaf students is that they learn language through visual rather than auditory modalities, they also have many similarities to hearing students. They have the same need to communicate and interact socially with others. Unfortunately, the majority of hearing people do not know sign language; and while many deaf people can visually read speech, many others who sign exclusively and adhere to deaf culture function best within the signing deaf community and are at significant disadvantages in hearing milieus. While deaf students often do not understand humor based on word play or sound, they do appreciate humor, and the deaf culture has its own inside jokes. Deaf students have equal interests in competing in sports and academics as hearing students do. They feel the same emotions as others. While they hug each other more and spend longer times on good-byes, their social interactions still fulfill the same needs for belonging, connection, and communication.

Blind students

Differences from sighted students
Blind students with normal hearing do not miss out on the auditory medium wherein children learn to understand and use speech and language as deaf students do. However, while they can learn spoken language normally, they cannot learn to read and write visually as other children can. They must learn Braille and have access to Braille publications to read and/or listen to books on tape. Today they have the added advantage of computer text-to-

speech software. Another significant difference is that blind students cannot learn their way around schools and other large, complex buildings simply through the experience of navigating them a few times. Sighted individuals often take this for granted. Blind students usually need help from Orientation and Mobility specialists to learn how to get around in indoor and outdoor settings. Without the benefit of the multitude of visual information others have, it can be very confusing not to know just which way to go, but even where one is and in what position relative to one's surroundings (orientation).

<u>Similarities to sighted individuals</u>
Although the totally blind cannot read printed text, blind students still often want to read and enjoy it. Some read available Braille texts by touch. Others listen to books on tape and/or use text-to-speech computer software, greatly expanding their options of available texts. Though blind students may not understand visual humor like sight gags, they still appreciate humor. Students not blind from birth have additional frames of reference for understanding visual expressions and comparisons. For example, Helen Keller, who became deaf-blind at 19 months, reportedly was told she had blue eyes and asked, "Are they like wee skies?" Without hearing or sight, Keller had to learn tactile finger-spelling to communicate, yet her accomplishments made her famous. A woman who became blind around nine years old found hilarious a coworker's description of another employee bundled up in a fur coat and hat with only her nose protruding. Blind people have the same social, communication, and emotional needs; they just need supplementary auditory information/verbal descriptions of what they cannot see.

Differences and similarities of physically disabled students

Physically normal students, and sometimes even educators, may not realize that even navigating through a school building—a seemingly simple everyday activity they take for granted—is not the same for the physically disabled. For example, buildings with traditional construction frequently include doorways too narrow for wheelchairs, solid obstacles impossible or difficult to move around, or stairs and grades not safely traversed using crutches. Federal legislation protecting the rights of the disabled has now mandated that all new constructions be accessible to them; however, this does not address old/existing buildings that often cannot be retrofitted. Also, physically disabled students have the same needs and desires to compete, win, and play as others, which should not be discounted. For example, wheelchair basketball and races are popular alternatives. In some schools, students in wheelchairs are also included in regular sports teams and games.

Family's role

Families play a critical role by frequently serving as their disabled child's first case manager. In this capacity, they are the most consistent and know the most about their child's abilities and needs. Families help coordinate the services disabled children need. They help them explore career possibilities and interests. They supply housing, transportation, adaptive equipment, and other necessities. When young people with disabilities progress from high school to college or employment and community living, their families support the transitions they must make. Families can help their children achieve greater understanding of themselves and their disabilities. However, many families do not realize how crucial such self-knowledge is, and many assume the schools teach this when they seldom do. Also, when educators and families avoid directly discussing disabilities and focus instead on abilities and strengths, children can grow up not realizing their disability's impact and the accommodations to facilitate their success. Students who avoid identification as disabled for fear of labeling and stigma are frequently unprepared for self-advocacy.

Understanding, communication, and disclosure of disability

Young people with disabilities will benefit by learning to understand themselves more fully; to understand their disabilities more completely; and to explain their disabilities more effectively to others. They will often need help from experts to make decisions whether to disclose their disability to others and to become more prepared for such disclosure. Even more importantly, young people with disabilities need to gain a better comprehension of how their opportunities in social, educational, and employment contexts can often be enhanced by disclosing their disabilities in certain situations. Where appropriate, disclosure of disability can give them access to services and accommodations they would not be entitled to if they were not disabled. Experts have prepared informational publications to support them in this issue. For example, the National Collaborative on Workforce and Disability for Youth (NCWD-Y) has published *The 411 on Disability Disclosure: A Workbook for Youth with Disabilities* to help youth and parents make informed decisions about disclosure and its various impacts.

Financial and service challenges on family systems

The challenges and demands on family systems are compounded when a member has a disability, and such challenges are typically long-term. Regardless of the type of family, the age of the disabled member, and the type of disability, many of the family demands are the same. For example, obtaining appropriate health services, social services, and educational services of sufficient quality often entail significant economic burdens, as do modifying the home to accommodate a disability and procuring adaptive equipment, medications, and special diets. Although families may qualify for public funding, e.g., from Medicaid, Social Security SSI, or private health insurance, additional challenges are not only to discover which programs and services their child is eligible for, but moreover to interact with various bureaucracies to confirm such eligibility—frequently on a repeated basis. Another major problem is service coordination among providers, like doctors, teachers, counselors, physical and occupational therapists, social workers, and dietitians. Frequently providers are not informed of one another's actions and may give contradictory information.

Impact on families

Emotional and caregiving
Caring for a disabled child or family member, particularly one with more severe disabilities, is a daily stressor that can exhaust caregivers and all family members emotionally and physically. Emotional stress includes anxiety, anger, guilt, and insecurity—about the disability's cause, other family members' needs, whether caregivers are doing enough, the future, etc. Families grieve the disabled member's functional losses, initially and recurrently. A member's disability frequently causes major changes in family life. Members, especially females, may discard or alter jobs and/or career plans for caregiving duties. Some members feel too involved in care while others feel left out, and within-family relationships change. Different loyalties and/or alliances develop within the family. Past research has found that while disability tended to increase marital tension, it did not necessarily increase divorce rates.

<u>Family resources, social roles, lifestyle, leisure time, and community interactions</u>
When a family member has a disability, it can deplete the family's resources in terms of money, time, and energy far out of proportion to other demands. This often detracts from meeting other needs of the family and its other members. The family members find they must change their lifestyle, for example, spending less money, time, and energy on leisure activities and staying at home more. Families may abandon their plans and dreams for the future because they no longer have enough of these resources to pursue them. Community members may exclude the disabled member and family; avoid them; and/or denigrate them with looks or comments. Though federal legislation mandates inclusion, many communities do not have the resources, facilities, and programs to enable full inclusion. Many families state they feel burdened not by the disabled member, but by rejection, judgment, stigmatization of the member and family, and other negative behaviors and attitudes—from not only strangers, but also service providers, friends, and relatives.

<u>Variation in the impact of disabilities on families</u>
Research shows the functioning and health of family members can be compromised by disability's additional demands. This includes elevated risks of behavioral and psychological symptoms in other family members. But despite this greater risk, studies also find that the majority of children and adults in families with a disabled member do not demonstrate such behavioral or psychological problems. This is attributed to the family members' adaptive abilities: they find and apply various coping skills to address the additional stresses caused in their life by the disability. Even though having a disabled member can cause families to experience grief, fatigue, depletion of resources, and other stressors, many families have also reported experiencing greater family closeness, acceptance of other people, new friendships, deepened spiritual faith, greater self-efficacy and sense of competence, more respect for life, and becoming stronger as a family. Thus, both negative and positive consequences are associated with having a family member with a disability.

<u>Differential psychosocial effects</u>
Families are affected differentially by the degree of a member's disability: its type, i.e., whether it is a motor, sensory, or cognitive disability; how visible the disability is; how much pain or other symptoms are involved; the disabled member's life expectancy or prognosis; how much treatment and/or care is required; and whether the disability is progressive, constant, or relapsing in nature. Some experts believe these characteristics have more influence on a chronic condition's psychosocial impact than the diagnosis itself. Constant disabilities, e.g., spinal cord injuries, necessitate major initial family restructuring, plus long-term endurance and persistence. While the family can plan for a known future, they can still become exhausted, especially if community resources are lacking. Progressive disabilities, e.g., dementia or degenerative arthritis, cause grief over continuous losses, uncertainty about living arrangements and degrees of dependency, and increasing demands in caretaking. Relapsing disabilities, e.g., cancer or epilepsy, require less continual care but more ability to shift suddenly from normal to crisis mode and rapidly activate resources.

<u>Differential impacts of cognitive or intellectual disabilities</u>
Research studies have shown that families appear to have more difficulty coping with cognitive or intellectual disabilities. Mental impairments can limit the disabled member's ability to assume responsible roles or to live independently, and/or increase the demands on families to be more vigilant to protect the disabled member. In cases of severe or profound intellectual disability, families may experience additional stress caused by boundary ambiguity—i.e., the disparity between the disabled member's physical and

psychological presence makes his or her membership in the family unclear to the other members, as the disabled member is present as a part of the family in some ways, but in other ways is absent or only partially present. The ambiguity of this situation causes families more stress, as it can be more difficult for them to plan the roles of the other family members when they do not know what they can expect.

Effects of medical advances

When the life expectancy of a disabled member is unclear, the family finds it harder to plan its members' future roles in life; to know future care costs; or, when the member needs help with daily living activities, to decide on optimal living arrangements. For example, individuals with Down syndrome often have congenital heart defects and died younger in the past, but with improved medical care, they now live longer. And between 1970 and 1991, the survival of American children with cystic fibrosis increased by 700 percent, from a median life expectancy of eight years to twenty-six years. This opens up new questions about marriage, procreation, and other difficult family choices. Ethical problems are also presented when medical advances can extend the lives of those with serious medical conditions. Considerations include weighing benefits versus costs, when and/or why to intervene and how aggressively. Family members may disagree about these. Moreover, courts and/or hospitals may prohibit chosen family actions. Such cases provoke much controversy (witness the 1998–2005 case of Terri Schiavo).

Considerations for families regarding functional status

A person's functional status is the extent to which s/he can perform activities of daily living (ADLs) like self-feeding, toileting, or walking. The severity of impairment in these activities caused by a disability can be assessed. The human help, support, and equipment an individual will require is inversely related to his/her functional status, and families are typically the main providers of such assistance. Providing it can constitute a burden for them, compromising their physical and mental health. For instance, research has found that parents and particularly mothers whose disabled children have lower functional status have more symptoms of depression. Another factor to consider is that when disabled children and their parents both grow older, and/or when grandparents are caregivers, their ability to provide the same amounts and durations of care can become more limited due to the physical stresses of caregiving, which may be unmanageable for many elderly persons.

Significance of age of disability onset and the age of parents at onset or diagnosis

In contrast to disabilities manifested in late adulthood, which are more predictable and less disruptive psychologically to families, disabilities occurring earlier in life are perceived as less normal, affect development more, and require making more adjustments for longer times. Congenital disabilities shape the identity and life of a child, so the child and family are not required to adjust to a sudden loss of function. An example is the difference between a child born with spina bifida versus a normal adolescent who sustains an injury and suddenly becomes paraplegic. Parental age at onset is also a factor in family response to disability. Adolescent parents still have salient developmental needs themselves; plus, they usually have fewer resources and less maturity for coping with the additional demands of their child's disability. Older parents have greater risks of bearing children with Down syndrome and other disabilities, lesser endurance for caregiving, and more fears about who will care for their child after their deaths.

Copyright © Mometrix Media. You have been licensed one copy of this document for personal use only. Any other reproduction or redistribution is strictly prohibited. All rights reserved.

Interrelationship of disability and child development

Because childhood development is sequential, the mastery of skills at each level or stage depends upon the successful completion of the previous stage. Therefore, the earlier in a child's life the onset of a disabling condition is, the more it interrupts the child's developmental progress. Accomplishing developmental tasks is complicated in many ways for children with disabilities. This influences what family roles the child can adopt and consequently affects the family. If an infant's disability prevents the infant from responding to parental efforts at nurturing, this impedes the development of bonding, secure attachment, and trust, undermining parenting competence. Toddlers must actively explore their social environments to develop self-control and autonomy. But sensory, motor, or cognitive disabilities can hamper such exploration. Parents may be overprotective for fear of additional damage or injury, and/or, due to guilt or sympathy, overindulgent. Others' negative feedback about the child's disability can reinforce these parental behaviors, additionally limiting the child's development of self-control and autonomy.

Challenges with attending school

As Freud, Erikson, Piaget, and others have observed, when children begin school, their social and emotional focus shifts from the parent-child relationship to developing social relationships outside of the home with peers, children of other ages, and adults other than parents. The focus of child development consequently shifts from mainly personal skills and parental attachment to social competencies and interpersonal skills. In spite of government mandates of special education and inclusion, schools still vary significantly in their effectiveness with these. Insufficient funding for special education programs; inadequate training of school staff for accommodating instruction to special needs; and frequently, negative attitudes regarding disabilities in school personnel and other children, constitute some of the obstacles faced by children with disabilities and their parents. Because of the variance among schools in this respect, some families realize great resources in school programs, while others realize great additional challenges in trying to advocate for their disabled children's educational rights with schools and other service providers.

Challenges of adolescent development

As especially elucidated by Erikson, adolescents have the developmental tasks of developing their individual identities, separating from their childhood relationships with parents, and becoming more independent. Having a disability makes these tasks more challenging for a teenager. While normally developing adolescents often engage in risk-taking, e.g., experimenting with alcohol and tobacco, as part of this process, teens with disabilities may refuse prescribed medications, diets, or other disability-related treatments as their form of the risk-taking part of the developmental process. The natural adolescent development of sexuality also involves additional complications for disabled teens, as they often experience anxieties and fears about their desirability, performance, and future potential for marriage and reproduction. The complications they encounter can include being exploited sexually by others for the cognitively disabled, risk of contracting sexually transmitted diseases, and possible higher risks of pregnancy for girls with disabilities.

Amphetamines for ADHD

Many adults do not understand why a child who is already hyperactive would be prescribed a stimulant drug, thinking this would only make them even more so. However, stimulants like amphetamines often have the effect of helping children with ADHD to focus their attention better for longer time periods. This compares to the effects of caffeine and controlled amphetamine doses in helping normal but tired adults concentrate better. Serious amphetamine side effects include rapid, uneven, or pounding heartbeat; burning or pain with urination; increased talkativeness; other unaccustomed behaviors; extremes of depression or elation; muscular twitches/motor tics; physical tremors; hallucinations; and dangerous elevations in blood pressure, with symptoms like buzzing in the ears, severe headaches, shortness of breath, cardiac arrhythmias, chest pain, confusion, anxiety, seizures, and others. Less serious side effects include blurred vision, dizziness, weakness, moderate headaches, irritability, restlessness, agitation, insomnia, dry mouth, bad taste in the mouth, constipation, diarrhea, stomachache, nausea, vomiting, fever, loss of appetite, weight loss, hair loss, loss of libido, and others.

Depakote

Depakote is an anticonvulsive prescribed to control seizures. It can sometimes cause pancreatitis or liver damage. If so, symptoms include jaundice, low-grade fever, pale/clay-colored stools, dark-colored urine, loss of appetite, upper stomach pain, nausea, and vomiting. Emergency medical attention should be pursued if the child has these symptoms. Additional serious side effects include agitation, anxiety, depression, hostility, mental or physical hyperactivity, restlessness, suicidal or self-injurious ideations, confusion, fainting, weakness, bruising easily, urine in the blood, body aches, swollen glands, other flu-like symptoms, decreased urination, excessive sleepiness, incoordination, nystagmus, double vision, painful skin, burning eyes, rashes with blisters and peeling, and other symptoms. Allergic reactions to Depakote cause symptoms of breathing difficulty, hives, and/or swelling of the throat, tongue, lips, or face. Less serious side effects include mild sleepiness, mild weakness, upset stomach, constipation, diarrhea, tremors, changes in vision, hair loss, an unpleasant/unusual taste in the mouth, and others. Educators should always know students are taking seizure medications. They should not first assume behavior or mental disorders or sleep deprivation.

Pulmozyme

A doctor may prescribe Pulmozyme to a patient who has cystic fibrosis. This condition causes thick mucus secretions in the lungs, interfering with normal breathing. Excessive DNA in the pulmonary secretions causes these symptoms. Pulmozyme is a synthesized protein that breaks down this extra DNA. It makes the lung secretions thinner and thus less likely to obstruct breathing, and also decreases the patient's risk of respiratory tract infections. Pulmozyme is given in solution via inhalation from a nebulizer. Allergic reactions to Pulmozyme cause symptoms like breathing difficulty, swelling of the face, lips, or tongue, hives, swelling/closing of the throat, chest pain, and/or fever. Emergency medical attention or immediate physician contact are indicated for these, which are the primary serious side effects. Less serious Pulmozyme side effects include changes in the voice; a sore throat; laryngitis; rashes; conjunctivitis, or red, irritated, or inflamed eyes; nasal congestion and/or discharge; and other symptoms, for which a doctor should be consulted.

Medications for childhood anxiety disorders

According to psychiatrists, children with anxiety are often prescribed the wrong medications when practitioners fail to understand the children's experiences and lack knowledge of evidence-based anxiety treatments. Anxious children have attentional difficulties, not from attention deficits but worries. They are often misdiagnosed as having ADHD and prescribed stimulants. These improve concentration, but not mood; they can even increase anxiety and the insomnia it causes. Alpha-two agonists, e.g., clonidine or guanfacine, lower arousal levels and can calm children, but do not treat their anxiety. Some practitioners even prescribe antipsychotics, also inappropriate for anxiety disorders. Serotonin-specific reuptake inhibitor (SSRI) antidepressants are most effective in research studies and patient treatments by experienced psychiatric physicians. These can improve children's anxiety relatively fast, e.g., beginning in a week or two, and are most effective in conjunction with cognitive-behavior therapy. Benzodiazepines (Valium, Librium, Dalmane, Halcion, Xanax, Ativan, etc.), used as anti-seizure treatments, sleep aids, and muscle relaxants as well as anxiolytics, also provide short-term help for extreme anxiety, but not long-term help like SSRIs.

Medications for childhood schizophrenia

While the symptoms of childhood schizophrenia can differ from adult symptoms, the same antipsychotic medications are prescribed to children as adults (though in different dosages), in conjunction with psychotherapy. A few of these drugs include Haldol, Thorazine, Stelazine, Mellaril, Risperdal, Loxitane, Moban, and lithium, which is also often prescribed for bipolar disorder. Antipsychotics in the phenothiazine class, such as Thorazine, Stelazine, and Mellaril, have significant risks of side effects like tardive dyskinesia, which refers to repetitive, involuntary movements that can be irreversible even upon discontinuing treatment; dystonias, like involuntary tongue thrusts, muscular rigidity, etc.; and extrapyramidal syndrome, involving muscle spasms, which are usually reversible on discontinuing treatment but may need other treatments to resolve when they are serious or interfere with breathing. Another side effect is pseudoparkinsonism, which mimics the symptoms of Parkinson disease including "pill-rolling" finger tremors, "mask-like" flat facial appearance, a shuffling gait, and muscular rigidity. A very serious side effect is neuroleptic malignant syndrome. Thorazine and other phenothiazines can also themselves cause psychiatric side effects.

Gabapentin

Although gabapentin is prescribed to adults for the nerve pain of shingles and for Restless Legs Syndrome, it is prescribed to children primarily for seizure disorders. For epilepsy, it is prescribed alone or with other medications to children at least 12 years old as well as adults, and with other medications to children aged 3–12 years for partial seizures. Caution is advised with patients having liver disease, kidney disease, or heart disease. Gabapentin can cause suicidal or self-injurious ideations in some patients. It can also cause depression, anxiety, changes in mood or behavior, agitation, hostility, restlessness, or physical or mental hyperactivity. Serious gabapentin side effects include increased instead of decreased seizures; fever, body aches, swollen glands, flu-like symptoms; bleeding or bruising easily; skin rashes; severe tingling, numbness, or pain; muscular weakness; chest pain, heart arrhythmia, shortness of breath; rapid weight gain, edema/swelling; less/no urination;

confusion; nausea, vomiting; worsened/new coughing; difficulty breathing; nystagmus; and upper stomach pain, loss of appetite, dark urine, and jaundice (signs of liver damage).

Gabapentin is prescribed to children to control seizures. It is also prescribed to adults for Restless Legs Syndrome and for nerve pain secondary to shingles. It may be prescribed to some children for whom other anti-seizure medications have not been effective. Some less serious side effects of gabapentin include sleepiness, dizziness, weakness, fatigue; constipation, diarrhea, nausea; blurred vision; headaches; swelling of the breasts; dryness of the mouth; and loss of coordination or balance. In children particularly, gabapentin is more likely to cause problems with memory, changes in behavior, difficulty concentrating, and restless, aggressive, or hostile behavior. If parents or caregivers observe any of these side effects in children who are taking gabapentin, they should always contact the prescribing physician. Educators should always ensure they are informed when students are taking seizure medications, especially younger children less likely to know/understand or volunteer this information. They should not automatically assume a child has an attention deficit or behavior disorder instead. They should also realize this is probably the reason if a student seems sleepy.

Medical needs for spina bifida

Spina bifida is a neural tube defect: the neural tube that will become the baby's brain, spinal cord, and enclosing tissues does not close completely. Of its several types, spina bifida occulta frequently needs no treatment. Spina bifida meningocele requires surgery to replace the meninges back into the spinal column and close the vertebral opening. Spina bifida myelomeningocele needs surgery within 24 to 48 hours of birth to lessen infection risk and protect the spinal cord from further trauma. Surgeons sometimes install a shunt in the infant's brain during surgery to control hydrocephalus, a buildup of fluid in the brain. Fetal surgery, before week 26 of gestation, reduces children's needs for brain shunts, crutches/walkers/braces, etc., but is risky for mothers and highly elevates premature birth risk. Despite early surgery, children with myelomeningocele often have lower-body paralysis and bladder and bowel problems. Treatment includes exercises preparing for later assisted walking. Myelomeningocele complications include tethered spinal cord from postoperative scar tissue, inhibiting growth. Surgery can restore some function and mitigate the extent of disability

Medical needs for muscular dystrophy

Muscular dystrophy, a genetic condition, makes muscle fibers unusually vulnerable to damage, causing progressive weakness. Symptoms include breathing/swallowing difficulties and limb contractures. Some forms affect the heart and other organs. Among at least seven forms of MD, the Duchenne type comprises roughly half of all cases and is most common in boys. Children learning to walk may fall often; have trouble getting up, running, and jumping; waddle when walking; and have enlarged calf muscles. They also often have learning disabilities. With no cure, treatment focuses on decreasing/preventing spinal and joint deformities and enabling mobility as long as possible. Prednisone and other corticosteroids can slow progression of some forms of MD and enhance muscular strength, but also weaken bones, elevating fracture risks, with long-term use. Surgeries can loosen contracted joints, correct spinal scoliosis to ease breathing, and install pacemakers for MD-related heart conditions. Range-of-motion exercises improve flexibility. Braces support weak muscles, stretch muscles and tendons, and preserve flexibility, slowing contracture progression. Some patients need C-PAP sleep apnea devices or ventilators.

Medical needs for cystic fibrosis

Children who inherit cystic fibrosis have a genetic defect that makes normally thin, slippery secretory juices become thick and sticky. These fluids, which normally lubricate the tissues, when thickened obstruct passageways, ducts, and tubes, particularly in the lungs and pancreas. CF has no cure, and treatment involves complex management. However, improved detection and intervention have decreased complications and ameliorated symptoms, allowing children to live longer. Treatment focuses on loosening and eliminating mucus from the lungs; preventing and controlling lung infections; preventing and treating intestinal obstructions; and supplying sufficient nutrition. This includes antibiotics; mucus-thinning medications; bronchodilators to keep airways open; pancreatic enzymes to improve nutrient absorption; chest clapping by hand or mechanical device, inflatable vibrating vests, and breathing masks/tubes; breathing exercises and strategies; nutritional counseling; energy-conserving techniques; counseling, and/or support groups. Additional procedures include oxygen therapy to prevent pulmonary hypertension, endoscopy and lavage to suction mucus, surgical nasal polyp removal, feeding tubes for supplemental nutrition, surgical removal of bowel obstructions, and lung transplants.

Treatments addressing medical needs of cerebral palsy

Damage or deficient development in the brain before birth usually causes cerebral palsy, which affects muscle tone, posture, and movement. It can include spasticity causing muscular rigidity and incoordination, athetosis causing involuntary movements and exaggerated reflexes, or both. Its effects can range from an unsteady gait or slight limp to complete loss of walking and speech, and every degree in between these. Botox can help isolated spasticity, and muscle relaxants can help generalized spasticity. CP patients benefit from physical therapy to improve motor development, mobility, strength, balance, and flexibility. Splints or braces can stretch stiff muscles, prevent contractures, and help some children walk. Occupational therapists provide adaptive equipment and alternate strategies to help children participate independently in daily routines and activities. Speech-language therapists help children speak clearly, use sign language or communication boards/devices, and improve eating/swallowing muscle use. Orthopedic surgery for severe deformities or contractures can reposition bones or joints; lengthen contracted tendons and muscles to reduce pain and increase mobility; and sometimes sever extremely spastic muscles.

Assessment and Program Planning

Reliability and validity

Reliability is consistency of an assessment instrument's data across repeated administrations. For example, reliable test scores are similar when the same test-taker is given the test two/three times at two-week intervals. Internal consistency reliability is consistency of test items with one another by measuring the same quantity/construct. Inter-rater consistency is reliability among individuals scoring the same test. Intra-rater consistency is an individual's consistency in rating responses to various test items. Validity is whether a test measures what it claims/intends to measure. Content validity means a test includes items representing the complete range of possible items. Construct validity means a test's scores measure the construct they are meant to measure, like intelligence. Criterion validity means a test's scores effectively measure a construct according to established criteria. Concurrent validity, a type of criterion validity, means a test measures the criterion and the construct at the same time. Predictive validity, another type of criterion validity, means test scores effectively predict future outcomes, as when aptitude tests predict future subject grades.

Generalizability, compensatory grading, noncompensatory grading, and cut score

Generalizability is related to reliability, i.e., the consistency of test scores over repeated administrations; but it moreover refers to the specific features of a certain test administration. It means the results on one test can be generalized to apply to other tests with similar formats, content, and operations. Generalizability can also refer to whether a test's results can be generalized from an individual or group to the larger population. Compensatory grading is the practice of balancing out lower performance in one area or subject with higher performance in another. Noncompensatory grading does not permit such balancing, but requires a similar standard of achievement in each area or subject. A cut score is a predetermined number used to divide categories of data or results from a test instrument. For example, a cut score can divide the categories of passing and failing scores. It can also divide the category of passing scores from a category of "honors" or "excellent" or "superior" scores.

Standard deviation, standard score, and scaled score

Standard deviation measures variability within a set of numbers. In interpreting assessment results, it measures how much scores among a group of test-takers vary around the mean/average. For example, a bell curve shows a normal distribution of test scores: the high center represents the majority of scores closest to the mean, while the lower sides represent standard deviations above and below it. SD is calculated by obtaining the square root of the sum of deviations of each score and the mean, and dividing this figure by the number of scores in the group. The standard score, or z score, represents the amount whereby an individual score deviates from the mean, measured in SDs. For example, a common SD unit for IQ tests is 15 where the mean is 100. A scaled score is obtained by converting a group of test scores to a scale/distribution with a designated mean and SD. For example, the U.S. Medical Licensing Examination (USMLE) has a mean of 200 and a SD of 20.

Domain and the Item Response Theory

In educational assessment, the term "domain" is the identified scope of expected learning to be assessed. Tests typically present students with samples of assessment tasks. The results of these tests are then interpreted to generalize the performance on the full range of possible assessment tasks that would measure the domain of intended learning. Item Response Theory (IRT) posits that performance on a test item is attributed to three influences: the item itself; the test-taker; and the interaction between the two. In education, when large groups of test-takers are given many test items to produce large data sets, raters can use formulae to separate influences on test items from the test-takers' true ability, skills, or knowledge. However, the kind of assessment that is normally conducted within a given educational program does not afford enough data to calculate parameters according to Item Response Theory that would be stable enough to be meaningful.

Mean, median, and mode

The mean is the average of a group of numbers, e.g., scores within a group of students taking the same test. Among six students, if one scores 50%; one 60%; one 70%; one 80%; one 90%; and one 100%, the sum of scores = 450; divided by 6 (students/scores) yields an average/mean of 75%. The median is the center-most score in a group. For example, if the range of student scores on a test is 65%, 75%, 80%, 85%, and 95%, then 80% = the middle/median. When there is an even number of scores, the median is the average of the two most central scores. For example, with four scores of 50%, 60%, 70%, and 80%, 60% and 70% are averaged for a median of 65%. The mode is the most frequent score in a set. If in a group of students, one scored 100% on a test; one, 95%; two, 90%; three, 85%; four, 80%; three, 75%; two, 70%; and one, 65%, the mode = 80%.

Positive skew, negative skew, and normal distribution

When the majority of a group of numbers, such as test scores, is concentrated toward the high end of the range/distribution with the minority "tail" of scores near the low end, this group of numbers is said to be positively skewed. When the majority of scores is bunched near the lower end of the distribution, with a minority "tail" near the higher end, the set of scores is negatively skewed. A normal curve is called a bell curve because it resembles the shape of a bell, with the largest number of scores collected around the center mean or average score and the numbers of scores descending as they move away from the center and mean. Parametric statistics assume a normal distribution. However, in typical educational assessments, the data obtained as scores on testing instruments are not usually found to be distributed normally.

SEM and Standard Error of the Mean

If an individual student took a lot of tests that were similar in size or length (i.e., the number of items on each test), the assessors can estimate how much that student's scores will vary. This estimate is called the Standard Error of Measurement (SEM). The SEM is calculated using the reliability coefficient that is established for a given test and the Standard Deviation (SD) that has been established for the group of scores that the student achieved. When a group of students takes a test, the assessors can estimate how much the mean or average score of that group would vary if they selected many samples with the same sizes and then calculated the means or averages of their scores. This estimate of variance around the mean of a group's test scores is called the Standard Error of the Mean.

Confidence Interval

Statisticians use the Confidence Interval to express the range wherein a "true" or "real" score is situated. The purpose is to acknowledge and address the fact that the measurement of a student's performance contains "noise," i.e., interfering/confounding variables that influence the measure of pure ability/achievement, akin to static in a radio, phone, or other sound signal. Giving a Confidence Interval shows the probability that a student's true score is within the range defined by that interval. For example, a student might take a test and receive a score of 80%. If that student took several other, similar tests, most likely the student's scores would not all be exactly 80%; they would be similar, but vary. The assessors might give a Confidence Interval of + 2 Standard Deviations, 95% of the time. Computing Confidence Intervals does not use Standard Scores (z scores), but literal scores to show the upper and lower limits of the range of likely scores.

Cut score

Educators use a cut score to determine which scores are passing and which are failing. They set a particular number as the cut score; all scores above it are passing and all scores below the cut score are failing. Using methods developed for multiple-choice tests allows them to adjust for various factors, e.g., the difficulty of a certain test or assessing student population with special needs, rather than arbitrarily assigning the same cut score to all tests. One such method for establishing a cut score is the Nedelsky method: the assessor(s) identify a "borderline" group of students, i.e., those who do not always pass or fail, but tend to score on the borderline of passing/failing. The assessor(s) estimate how many of these "borderline" students will probably answer a given test item correctly. A common number for this group is 10 students. The sum of the percentages of students estimated to respond correctly to each test item is rounded to an integer, yielding the cut score.

Angoff method for determining a pass/fail cut score
To determine which scores on a given test are passing or failing, educators can use several established methods. In the Angoff method, one or more assessors select a group of "borderline" students (i.e., those not always passing or failing but with equal chances of either) and estimate which choice(s) in a multiple-choice test item these students could eliminate as an incorrect answer and what percent of the choices left these students would guess as correct. For example, if they might eliminate one choice of five as wrong, their probability of guessing the right choice from the four choices left is 25% (1/4). The assessors add up the percentages for all of the test items and round the sum to an integer, which would be the cut score for that test. In the modified Angoff procedure, the assessors also estimate how many of the students would fail the test, and if they deem it necessary, they modify their estimations to produce a number of failures they find more reasonable.

Ebel method for determining a pass/fail cut score
Rather than arbitrarily setting the same pass/fail cut score for all tests, several methods exist for determining an appropriate cut score for a particular instrument. The Ebel method considers the importance and difficulty level of each test item in establishing a cut score for a test. First the testers divide all test items into six categories: High, Medium, and Low importance; and High, Medium, and Low difficulty. Then, after selecting a group of

"borderline" students who do not always pass or fail tests but are about equally likely to do either, they estimate how many of these students would probably get each item correct in each of these six categories. They add up their estimated percentages for each test item and round the sum to an integer, which is the cut score. The assessors can also then modify their estimations based on data they may obtain from a student class or group's actual test results.

<u>Hofstee method to determine pass/fail cut scores</u>
Several methods have been developed to set a cut score, the score above which all scores are passing and below which all scores are failing, for a particular test with a multiple-choice format. The Hofstee method is also called the compromise method. It addresses the difference between norm-referenced and criterion-referenced tests, i.e., tests that compare individual student scores to the average scores of a normative sample of students found representative of the larger population versus tests that compare student scores to a pre-established criterion of achievement. Educators estimate an acceptable number of students who would fail the test and the largest number of test items a student who fails the test would answer correctly. They then plot the answers to this number of items plus two more on the cumulative score distribution. This allows them to determine how many items students could miss and how many failed test items would affect the number of students who could fail.

Norm-referenced tests and criterion-referenced tests

In reference to testing large groups, like the entire student body of a school, district, or state, the high-stakes standardized tests given are typically norm-referenced tests; that is, they compare students' scores to a normative sample of students deemed representative of the general population. Criterion-referenced tests may or may not be standardized and compare student scores to a predetermined set of criteria for acceptable performance. In the context of educational programs, norm-referenced tests seek to determine the highest or lowest achievement rather than the absolute score achieved. For example, educators might determine the 10 highest student scores on a certain test to reinforce with "best in group" awards. In this context, measures of mastery learning are examples of criterion-referenced or domain-referenced testing. Educators establish a minimum performance level score that equates to passing. Student scores are compared against this score, so the students in a given class could all pass or all fail the test.

Formative assessments versus summative assessments

Formative assessments are given during a lesson, unit, course, or program. Their purpose is to give the teachers and students an idea of how well each student is learning what the teacher has planned and expected for them to learn. The teacher uses the results of formative assessments to explain to each student his/her strengths and weaknesses, and how s/he can build on the strengths and improve the weaknesses, and to report student progress to parents, administrators, and others. Summative assessments are given after a lesson, unit, course, or program has been completed. Their purpose is to determine whether the student has passed the segment of instruction. This determines whether they need to repeat the instruction or can move on to successive segments. Summative assessments apply to lessons or units within a class, to courses in a subject, to promotion from one grade level to the next, and to graduation.

Item analysis

Item analysis is often used to evaluate test items that use multiple-choice formats to show the quality of the test item and of the test overall. Item analysis has an implicit orientation of being norm-referenced rather than criterion- or domain-referenced. That is, it evaluates test items using performance within the group of test-takers rather than an externally preset criterion for expected achievement. Characteristics analyzed in test items include how many high-scoring students got an item correct; how many low-scoring students got the item correct; the test item's discrimination index for separating high- and low-scoring test-takers; the test item's difficulty index; how many test-takers chose each of the answer choices on each test item; the quality of the correct answer choices; and the reliability of the test, i.e., how consistent its results are across separate administrations to the same test-takers.

Discrimination Index and Difficulty Index

The discrimination index is a measure of how well a specific test item can separate students who generally score high on the test from students who generally score low on it. Educators obtain a point biserial correlation between high total scores and low total scores with correct or incorrect item responses. Typically, they use total test scores to select the top 27% and bottom 27% of test-takers to magnify the variation between high and low test performance. When analyzing standardized, norm-referenced tests, the preferred discrimination index is .50. The difficulty index is a simple measure of how difficult a test item is considered. It is obtained by calculating the percentage of all students taking a test who answered a certain test item correctly.

Sensitivity and specificity and the KR20 formula

Sensitivity refers to how well a test identifies every member of a defined group. The more sensitive a test is, the more likely it can include some individuals who should not be in that group. Specificity refers to how well a test identifies only those members of a defined group. The more specific a test is, the more likely it will omit some individuals who should be included in that group. Among many KR formulas used to estimate statistically a test's reliability or consistency, the KR20 is one that assumes that the relative difficulty of items on a test, and the correlations among those items, are basically equal. The KR20 formula deducts the variances of all individual test items from the total test's variance, which produces an estimate of the test's internal consistency reliability. When a test has items of dissimilar difficulty, the Horst's modification can be used to correct for this by estimating the maximal variance possible within a given range of item difficulties for that test.

Modified assessments of students with special needs on standardized tests

Exclusive of actual test items, in some states the test administration instructions may be clarified or simplified. Other than item responses, students may be allowed to highlight or make other marks in their test booklets. Students may be tested in small groups rather than whole class settings. Test administrators may give students additional time within the testing day to complete a test. Individual students may be tested separately with direct examiner supervision. Students with visual impairments may use visual magnifiers for test text, and hearing-impaired students may use audio amplification. Individual study carrels/enclosures may be used as noise buffers for hearing-impaired or distractible students. Special lighting, acoustics, special furniture, or adaptive furnishings may be allowed. Masking or colored overlays may be used to sustain student visual attention. American Sign Language (ASL) or Manually Coded English (MCE) may also be used to give test instructions (but not test items) to deaf, hard-of-hearing, or nonverbal students.

Some states allow students to mark their test responses in their test booklets, and then the school personnel transfer these onto the standardized answer form used by other students to be electronically scored. For students with vision, hearing, manual, or motor impairments, they may dictate their responses to multiple-choice test items aloud or in American Sign Language (ASL) or Manually Coded English (MCE) to a designed scribe who writes, types, or fills in bubbles, circles choices, or otherwise marks the student's answers on a form. For essay questions, some students may be permitted to use word processing software programs, with the spell-check and grammar-check features disabled. Other students may be allowed to dictate their essay answers orally to a voice recorder or scribe, or manually in sign language to an interpreter/scribe, or using speech-to-text computer software. In these cases, students supply all writing conventions of spelling and grammar in their dictation. Assistive devices that allow independent student work may be used.

For blind or visually impaired students or those with visual processing deficits, testers may provide Braille transcriptions of the printed test; large-print versions of the test; or, if the student needs larger type than the fonts used in large-print versions, test items may be enlarged. Students who require additional time and/or shorter testing durations (e.g., those with cognitive impairments, attention deficits, or behavior disorders) may be allowed to take a test normally administered in one sitting over more than one day and/or take supervised breaks during one test section. Medication effects and fluctuating attention and/or performance levels can be addressed by administering tests at the optimal time of day for the student. Examiners may test some students in homes or hospitals. Test items and answer choices may be presented in sign language, audio recordings, or read aloud. On math and science tests, like in fifth grade, some students may be allowed to use calculators and/or concrete math manipulatives.

Modified assessment procedures for ELL or ESL students

Students whose native language is not English are allowed some variations by the U.S. states to participate in standardized testing in the English language on a more equable footing with native English speakers. For example, they may hear the printed test instructions translated into their native language and read aloud. They may be allowed to ask questions in their native language to clarify test instructions. ESL/ELL students may be granted additional, supervised breaks during a testing day or test portion, providing they complete the portion within the testing day. (Standardized tests typically display a "STOP" sign to indicate the ends of test portions.) Students learning English may be allowed to take tests separately in groups with other ELL/ESL students, under supervision by school personnel cleared for test security, particularly if their regular instruction and/or testing have included similar flexibility. ELL/ESL students taking math and science tests may be permitted access to word lists or glossaries translated from English to their native language, excluding formulae or definitions.

General adaptions to assessments for special-needs students

General testing adaptations include using these oral directions interchangeably: "Find," "Show me," "Point to," and "Give me." Testers should place stimulus cards and manipulatives however the student is best able to perceive these. Concrete materials should be set on surfaces with boundary edges so they cannot roll away or fall down when students use them. Testers should arrange the test environment to eliminate or reduce distractions for students more susceptible to these. For visually impaired students, testers may enlarge stimulus cards as needed. They may replace visual stimuli with Braille, beeping objects or other auditory stimuli, or textured materials if the student is accustomed to using these regularly. Testing teachers can cut out the outlines of shapes or figures from stimulus cards. They may substitute spoken cues like "Tell me" instead of "Show me." As necessary, they may describe the content of pictorial stimuli. They should let students handle concrete objects as is needed. Students who wear corrective glasses should always wear these during assessments.

Teachers can allow students to use augmentative communication devices for receiving and responding to test stimuli. For students who use American Sign Language (ASL) or manually coded English, teachers should use these languages or have an interpreter use them instead of spoken instructions or stimuli whenever appropriate. Nonverbal students should be allowed to give test responses using vocalizations, gestures, or movements instead of speech. Some students may draw pictures instead of writing. (This can also apply to students with dyslexia.) As is appropriate, teachers may accept eye gazes as responses instead of speech or gesture. Students who wear hearing aids must wear them during assessments; teachers should check that they work first. Students with sensorimotor impairments should be given longer times to initiate responses. Teachers should accept changes in facial expressions or muscle tone as observed behaviors. Teachers should stabilize and position students to afford the most controlled possible motions. Teachers should also let students direct others to perform physical tasks.

Technological development of portfolio assessments

Just as physical portfolios show a student's work and creative products accumulated over time, ePortfolios store documents and photos of products and can be shared with others; but given the advent of social networks, they benefit from additional advantages of immediate communication and reinforcement. Digital archives can portray a student's life, from birth through early childhood family learning via scrapbooks, and through formal schooling and into employment and professional development. In portfolios, key processes include collecting products for the digital archive; selecting those demonstrating certain standards or goals by creating hyperlinks for others, which leads to reflecting or metacognition, helping the student construct meaning from the works s/he selected, aided by new storytelling models generated by technology; directing or goal-setting; presenting ePortfolios; and getting feedback on them. Social networking includes processes of connecting with others; listening to or reading posts; responding by commenting on posts; and sharing via linking or tagging. Key processes technology enables include archiving; linking and thinking; digital storytelling; collaborating; and publishing.

Students can be internally motivated (self-directed by inner goals) or externally motivated by outer rewards. The ePortfolios enabled by technology can support students' internal motivation and autonomy by establishing online environments wherein others feel good about participating, keeping systems relatively open, and giving users freedom to participate. Social networks support student autonomy by giving them choices and voices in the content they post and view; opportunities to share and give feedback; and far greater immediacy in all of their interactions. Students can experience academic and personal mastery through social networking, which affords the motivational factors of what Csikszentmihályi called "flow" (energized, positive, task-aligned, spontaneous, single-minded, focused, immersed, joyful, deep, and total engagement in an activity); the ability to showcase their achievements; and the benefits of enhanced self-insight and self-awareness. Via choice and personalization, students find their passions and voices. Constructing ePortfolios also helps students develop senses of purpose by engaging in something beyond themselves, understanding the relevance of what they learn, and seeing the "big picture."

Screening to identify students who need special education services

Screening is the important first step of the assessment process mandated by federal laws. All newborns should be screened for developmental disabilities, and children should continue to be screened through early childhood, preschool, and school years. While more obvious disabilities like spina bifida, cerebral palsy, Down syndrome, autism, multiple disabilities, or severe sensory impairment are detected early, others like learning disabilities, ADHD, and some behavior disorders often go unidentified until school. Public schools typically conduct periodic screenings of large student groups from grades K–3. Very low standardized achievement test scores can lead to referral for formal evaluation—only with written parental consent—to identify possible disabilities. Also, students' parents, teachers, and other school staff may identify students with suspected disabilities, as when they evidence behavioral or academic difficulties in classrooms. Some students are not identified with disabilities until higher grades, due to ineffective screening, referral, assessment, and/or identification procedures; to disabilities acquired later through injury, illness, etc.; or to problems not apparent until school demands surpass student coping skills.

Problems and solutions with school-based screening

While school screenings are vital and the process of identifying students with disabilities has a basic structure, there are no uniform or standardized sets of checklists, procedures, or testing instruments to identify disabilities in most students. The kinds of referral processes and tests utilized vary, both across and within states. According to educational experts, two main problems with screening procedures are over-identification and under-identification of disabilities. Research studies have shown that students have been over-identified with learning disabilities, while students with behavior disorders are under-identified, especially compliant students who are not aggressive or disruptive but have problems like social isolation, depression, or school phobia. Educators have been improving screening procedures to resolve these problems. For example, Walker et al (1990) created the Systematic Screening for Behavioral Disorders with three steps: first, teachers rank students according to designated criteria; then select the three highest ranked students and complete checklists to quantify their observations about them; and school psychologists/counselors observe identified students prior to any formal evaluation referrals.

Prereferral interventions

Prereferral interventions are a frequent practice intended to better the process of identifying students with disabilities by decreasing referrals to special education services and give regular education teachers more assistance and advice. Rather than first referring a student for evaluation to diagnose a possible disability, teachers initially try to address behavior or learning problems in the classroom through modifications. Only if modifications are found inadequate to the student's difficulties, and the teacher believes special services may be required, does s/he initiate the referral process. Most states in the U.S. require or recommend prereferral intervention in some form. One approach uses Teacher Assistance Teams (TATs). TATs usually comprise four members: the referring teacher and three other teachers. These teams provide teachers with a forum to meet, discuss, and brainstorm ideas to instruct students and/or manage them. Another approach is collaborative consultation. Specialists like speech-language pathologists work directly with referring teachers in planning, implementing, and evaluating instruction for students identified in regular education classrooms.

Identification through Child Find, referral, or request for evaluation

Under the federal IDEA law, each U.S. state is held responsible for locating, identifying, and evaluating all children in that state as having disabilities and in need of special education and related services. To carry out this mandate, the states engage in Child Find processes. This is one way that children are identified with disabilities. The state's Child Find system may ask a child's parents for permission to evaluate the child, or parents can contact the Child Find system themselves and request evaluation of their child. Another way children are identified is by referral. A teacher or other school professional suspecting a student might have a disability may request, in writing or orally, the student's evaluation. Parents must give consent before the evaluation can be made. The law also stipulates that a requested evaluation be within a reasonable time after receiving parental consent. Parents who suspect disability in their child may also request that the school evaluate the child.

Evaluation and eligibility determination

After screenings and prereferral interventions have been completed and a student is referred for formal evaluation or evaluation is requested, professionals must evaluate all developmental/learning areas related to the disability suspected. Test results are applied to decisions regarding eligibility for special education and related services, and an appropriate educational program. If parents disagree with evaluation results, they have the right under the IDEA to arrange an Independent Educational Evaluation (IEE) and to request payment for this evaluation by the school system. Once evaluation results have been collected and reported, parents meet with teachers and other qualified professionals to review them. They decide together whether the student meets the IDEA definition of a "child with a disability." Parents are entitled under the law to request a hearing challenging the eligibility decision if they disagree. If the child is found eligible for special education and related services, an IEP team must meet within 30 calendar days of eligibility determination to write an IEP.

First IEP meeting after eligibility is determined

After a student is determined eligible for special education and related services according to the IDEA, the school must schedule the first meeting to write an Individualized Education Program (IEP) for the student. The IDEA mandates that ALL students that receive special education and related services must have an IEP written for them. By this law, the school system must contact the parents and all others who are to participate in the IEP process. They must inform the parents early enough to ensure they are able to arrange to attend the meeting. They must schedule the meeting at a place and time with which the parents and the school agree. They must inform the parents of the purpose of this meeting and its location, date, and time. They must also inform the parents who else will be attending the meeting. The school staff is also to inform the parents that they may invite any other people to the IEP meeting who have special expertise or knowledge about their child.

In the first IEP meeting for a student, the IEP team includes the student, the parents, the student's teacher(s), specialists, other school personnel who interact with the student; outside consultants if invited; and any others with knowledge about the student, invited by the parents. If a group other than this IEP team decides placement for the student, the parents must also be included in that group. Parents must give consent before initial provision of special education and related services. With this consent, services must commence as soon as possible following the first IEP meeting. When parents disagree with the content of the IEP and/or their child's placement, they can discuss this with other IEP team members and work toward solutions. If the parents still disagree, they may request mediation or the school can offer mediation services. Parents also have the right to file complaints with the state education agency and to request a due process hearing. Mediation must be made available at this hearing.

IEP implementation

Once the IEP team has met and developed an IEP for a student and the parents agree with it, the school must give them a copy of the IEP. Each teacher and service provider working with the student can access the student's IEP and must know his/her specific duties in implementing the IEP. The school must ensure that the IEP is implemented as it is written, including providing all accommodations, modifications, and supports to the student as specified in the IEP document. As outlined in the IEP, the school must measure the student's progress toward yearly IEP goals. The school regularly informs the parents of their child's progress and whether it is sufficient for meeting the annual goals. Progress reports must be provided at least as frequently as those reporting nondisabled students' progress. IEPs are reviewed at least annually—more if the parents or the school request it. The IEP is revised if needed. Parents must be invited to review meetings, can suggest changes, and agree/disagree with IEP goals and/or placement.

Legal requirements for reevaluation in IEP process

All students receiving special education and related services are required by law to have an Individualized Education Plan (IEP). It is developed by the IEP team, which includes the student, parents, teachers, other school employees, other professionals, and any others invited by parents or schools who have contributions relevant to the student and his/her education. The student has received a formal evaluation to determine eligibility. The IEP is reviewed at least annually or more often if the school or parents request it and is revised as needed. Additionally, the student must be reevaluated at least every three years. Educators often call such reevaluation a "triennial." Reevaluation is made to determine whether the student still meets the IDEA definition of a "child with a disability" or not, and to reexamine the educational needs of the student. The three-year interval is a minimum, though: if circumstances indicate it, and/or if the parents or teachers request a new evaluation, the student must be reevaluated sooner than after three years.

Legally required information in IEP

Current performance, annual goals, and special education and related services
The IDEA requires the IEP to state the student's "present levels of educational performance," i.e. the student's current progress in school. Results of evaluations made to determine eligibility for special services; classroom tests and in-class and homework assignments; and observations contributed by parents, teachers, related service providers, and other school personnel provide the information for the statement of the student's current school performance. This statement includes the impacts of the student's disability on his/her progress and engagement in the school's general education curriculum. Annual goals are those the student can reasonably attain within a school year. These are subdivided into short-term objectives, or benchmarks. Goals can be academic, behavioral, social, or physical. Goals must be measurable to show if the student has met them. The IEP must name all special education and related services to be provided to or on behalf of the student, including supplementary services and aids; changes to the program; and training, professional development, or other provisions supporting school staff in providing services to the student.

Student's participation with nondisabled students, participation in statewide and district-wide testing; and dates and locations of services
All students identified with disabilities and eligible for special education and related services must have IEPs (Individualized Education Programs). The IEP must include an explanation of the degree, if any, to which the student will NOT be participating with nondisabled students in regular classrooms and other school activities. Regarding statewide and district-wide standardized achievement tests regularly given by school systems to students at certain age or grade levels, the IEP must identify which modifications in test administration the student will need. Moreover, if any such test is deemed inappropriate for a particular student, the student's IEP must explain why and state what alternative testing will be substituted. The student's IEP must also state when the student's special education and related services will start, how often services will be provided, in what locations services will be given, and the duration of the services.

Transition services, student's reaching the age of majority, and progress measurement
While a student reaches the age of 14—or sooner when applicable—the student's IEP must include in its pertinent sections which courses the student must take to attain his/her postschool goals. Every IEP following this must also contain a statement of the student's needs in transition services. Transition may be to postsecondary education; job training; and/or community living. When the student is 16 years old—or before if appropriate—the IEP must define which transition services the student will need as preparation for exiting the current school program/system. At least one year before the student reaches the age of majority, his/her IEP must state the student has been informed of any rights that will transfer from parents/caregivers to him/her. This only applies in states where rights are transferred when minor children reach majority age. Law requires the IEP to state how the

school will measure the student's educational progress and how it will inform the student's parents of their child's progress.

Additional content school systems and states may include in IEPs

While the IDEA federally mandates certain content in students' IEPs, individual states and school systems have much flexibility regarding what other information they require. Since federal law dictates that school districts document their compliance with federal requirements, some states and school systems choose to add information in their students' IEPs that serves to document their compliance with both federal and state laws. In general, some examples of additional elements IEPs can contain that document this compliance include: documentation that the school held the meeting(s) for writing, reviewing, and revising when necessary the student's IEP on a timely basis; documentation that the school furnished the student's parents with a copy of their legally mandated procedural safeguards and rights; documentation that the school has placed the student in the least restrictive environment possible where s/he can experience adequate learning and progress; and documentation that the school received parental consent to provide their child with evaluations, special education, and related services.

Key members of the IEP team

Members of a student's IEP team are not limited to, but include: the student; the parents; the special education teacher(s); specialist(s) or other service provider(s); the regular education teacher(s); someone able to interpret evaluation results; a representative of the school system; a representative of a transition services agency; and others having special expertise/knowledge about the student. (Sometimes an individual member fulfills more than one of these functions.) Parents are important team members for knowledge of their child, including his/her strengths and needs and their ideas about how to improve his/her education. Parents can contribute insights about their child's learning style and processes, what academic and life areas are of particular interest to their child, and other things only parents know about their children. Parents can consider other team members' recommendations about areas to focus on in school and can share their own suggestions. Additionally, parents can report to the school whether their child is applying skills s/he has learned in school, at home, and in other settings outside school.

The IEP team member who can interpret evaluation results can not only explain to other members what test results signify, e.g., the type of disability and deficit areas, but moreover how to design instruction appropriate to the student and characteristics identified by evaluation results. Skillfully interpreting test results informs the team how the student is currently faring in school and helps them pinpoint areas of particular student needs. This member's role is not only understanding and explaining test results, but furthermore explaining the instructional implications of those results and helping plan accordingly suitable instruction. The school system representative contributes extensive knowledge about teaching students with disabilities and about the special education services available in the school system. This member can discuss the school resources the student and educators will need. It is also important for this individual to have the authority for committing school system resources, and the ability for assuring all services specified in the IEP are actually provided to the student and staff.

If a special education student participates in regular education at all (which is increasingly the case these days), at least one of the student's regular education teachers must be included in the IEP team. This teacher can inform other team members about the regular classroom's general curriculum, and also what kinds of services, changes in the educational program, and/or aids would help the student to learn and succeed best. S/he can also suggest strategies for managing classroom behavior if this is an issue. The regular education teacher can also talk with the rest of the team about which supports the school staff will need to help the student progress toward annual IEP goals, engage in regular curriculum and succeed in it, participate in extracurricular activities, and be included in instruction with both nondisabled and disabled peers. Such school staff supports can include additional training, professional development, etc., not only for teachers but also administrators, cafeteria staff, bus drivers, and all others providing services to students with disabilities..

Informed by her/his training and experience in special education, the special education teacher contributes to the IEP team by discussing various topics. These include how to make adaptations and modifications to the general education curriculum that will enable the student to learn in the regular education setting; which supplementary services and aids the student is likely to require for succeeding in regular classrooms and other places; techniques for modification of assessments that enables the student to better demonstrate what s/he has learned; and additional elements of individualizing the instruction according to the unique needs of the student. Special educators not only help write IEPs; they are also responsible for working with students to implement them. They may do this in special education classes or resource rooms; team-teach with regular education teachers; and collaborate with regular education teachers and other school personnel, contributing expertise to meet the student's individual needs.

Parents and/or school system employees can invite individuals to participate as members of a student's IEP team based on their especial expertise and/or knowledge about the student. For instance, parents may know a professional with specific expertise in the student's particular disability; an advocate who has a relationship with the student; or a vocational educator who has been working with the student on employment skills. Such individuals are able to discuss the student's individual strengths and needs. The school system may also invite individuals, like paraprofessionals or professionals specializing in related services, who can contribute special expertise and/or knowledge about the student. A significant aspect of IEP development is the related services a student often needs; therefore, professionals specializing in such related services are frequently members or participants in the IEP team. These professionals can include physical therapists; occupational therapists; adaptive physical education instructors; orientation and mobility specialists; ASL interpreters; speech-language pathologists; psychologists; and others.

Material reviewed to determine special education and services needed

To develop the IEP, the team reviews evaluation results including individual tests given to the student to determine eligibility for services; classroom tests the student has taken; and the observations of parents, teachers, related service providers, paraprofessionals, administrators, and others involved. These help the team characterize the "present levels of educational performance" of the student, i.e., how s/he is currently functioning in school. They develop yearly goals targeting areas of educational need identified through this information. Information specific to the student they discuss includes the student's strongest assets; recent evaluation and/or re-evaluation results; parents' ideas to improve the student's education; and the student's performance on district-wide and statewide standardized examinations. The team's discussion of what the student needs should be guided by how they can help the student progress toward meeting yearly goals; engage in the general education curriculum and make progress in it; be included in participation and education with other students, both with and without disabilities; and participate in nonacademic and extracurricular activities.

Legal requirements regarding a student's placement

Once an IEP team has developed and written a student's IEP, where this program will be implemented—i.e., the student's placement—must also be decided. In some U.S. states, the IEP team is also the group that makes placement decisions. In others, a different group may decide student placements. However, in every instance the parents have the legal right to participate as members of the group deciding placement. Placement decisions must abide by the IDEA's requirements for the Least Restrictive Environment (LRE): students with disabilities must be educated together with students without disabilities to the maximum degree possible and fitting. In addition, the IDEA specifies that students with disabilities may only be removed from the regular school setting—to special classes or separate schools—if the severity and/or nature of the student's disability makes education in regular classes, including the use of supplementary services and aids, impossible to attain with satisfactory results.

Integrating affective, social, and life skills into academic curricula

Many students with disabilities need special education and support to learn daily living skills. With proper instruction, they can obtain and keep meaningful jobs and live in the community; but without specialized instruction, they frequently lose jobs and/or home placements. Life skills include proper attire, grooming, and hygiene; acceptable table manners; financial decision-making; and utilizing transportation to employment. Instruction in financial skills is required by some states, including counting money and making change; managing bank accounts; keeping personal budgets and records; making personal financial decisions; spending and using credit responsibly; estimating and paying taxes; paying bills; and renting/leasing. Household management includes housekeeping; meal preparation; doing/hiring home maintenance/repair; and new appliance warranty registration. Personal care includes obtaining health care, eschewing substance abuse; recognizing common illnesses, knowing prevention and treatment; and nutrition, physical fitness, and weight maintenance. Safety awareness includes recognizing safety/hazard signs, rules, and procedures; unfamiliar sounds and/or smells; and knowing emergency evacuation procedures. Buying, storing, planning, preparing, and eating balanced, appropriate meals are included.

In addition to skills in dress, hygiene, other personal care, finance, household management, safety awareness, and food preparation, students with disabilities must also receive instruction, integrated into academic curricula in school, in how to purchase and care for clothing. They must be instructed in responsible citizenship, including knowing their own civil rights and responsibilities; obtaining legal aid; reporting crimes; for males, registering with Selective Service at age 18; knowing and obeying laws; knowing about federal, state, and local governments; and voting. Disabled students must also learn about community resources available; how to select and plan leisure activities, appreciate their importance, and participate in them; to plan vacation activities and social events; and practice music, arts, crafts, hobbies, and sports. Students must also be instructed in community navigation, including knowing right from left and front from back; safety and traffic rules; carpooling and other transportation; reading maps; and when applicable, learning to drive and obtaining a driver's license and automobile insurance. Special and regular educators, families, and peers provide instruction.

Special student factors

The law requires a number of "special factors" for the IEP team to consider as applicable with individual students. If a student's behavior impedes his/her and/or other students' learning, the team must consider effective, positive behavioral supports and intervention techniques to manage, control, or change the behavior. If the student has limited English-language proficiency, the team must consider the student's linguistic need relative to his/her IEP. If a student is blind or visually impaired, the team must provide Braille texts or instruction in Braille, or determine through evaluations the student does not need such instruction. In the latter case, the team must specify any other methods and/or devices the student needs and provide these. The team must consider any communication needs a student may have. For deaf or hard-of-hearing students, the team must consider their communication and linguistic needs, including opportunities for communicating directly with peers and staff in ASL or their other customary communication method(s). The team must also consider any student needs for assistive technology services and/or devices.

Different program placement and integration into placement

A student's IEP may be implemented in various placement settings according to the individual student's needs. Settings include placement in the regular education class, with supplementary services and aids the student needs; in a special class for all or part of the school day, with other students all also receiving special education and related services; in a special school dedicated to students needing special education and related services; in a hospital; in an institutional facility; and other settings. To fulfill its legal requirements to make sure a student is placed appropriately, a school system can take various actions. For example, it may furnish the student with a suitable program as part of the school system. Or it may contract with an outside agency that can provide the student with an applicable program. Or it may make some other arrangements and/or make use of other mechanisms available to pay for or otherwise provide the student a program appropriate and consistent with the terms of the IDEA.

Prioritizing areas of the general education curriculum for students with disabilities

The IDEA and NCLB require all students' access to general education curriculum. Educators can help disabled students by connecting academic content to real-life activities. Achievement standards include the same academic content, but utilize alternate performance indicators still fitting content standards for reading and math. While alternative assessment methods and definitions of achievement standards vary considerably across states, educators in all states must provide instruction effective in helping students with disabilities meet standards. Teachers in some states select which responses are assessed to document progress toward state standards—e.g., portfolio assessments; specific choice-making; sight words; task analyses; generalized responses, like requests; problem-solving; and self-initiation responses. Systematic prompting with feedback, reinforcement, correction, and fading is an instructional support method. In general education settings, systematic instruction to small mixed-ability groups; cooperative learning groups; trials embedded in general education lectures/lessons; observational learning; peer tutors; and self-instruction and problem-solving materials are options. Assistive technology aids symbol use, and can reduce behavior problems and increase social interaction. Special and general educator planning collaboration is vital.

Learning Environments and Instructional Practices

Impact of teachers' attitudes and behaviors on student achievement outcomes

Research studies show that when teachers establish supportive relationships with their students; communicate clearly and consistently enforce high expectations of their students academically and behaviorally; and deliver a high quality of pedagogy and instruction to their students, the students are more likely to develop attitudes and behaviors of engagement in their learning, and perceptions of their own academic competence. These student attitudes and behaviors are found in turn to augment student achievement in key academic areas like reading and math. Experts define students' engagement as how much inherent interest they demonstrate in school, and the quantity and quality of their participation in schoolwork. This engagement and participation include both attitudes, like positive values about learning, motivation, interest, enthusiasm, and pride in succeeding, and also behaviors like attention, effort, and persistence. Therefore, students who are engaged pursue activities in and out of classrooms that further learning and/or succeeding. Additionally, they demonstrate curiosity, desire for more knowledge, and emotionally positive responses to school and learning.

Expectations and student behavior

Researchers have found that teachers are often unprepared for problem behaviors from both nondisabled and disabled students in urban school settings. Some reasons for such problem behaviors include the higher proportions in urban school populations of students from lower socioeconomic levels; of students from families who do not speak English; and of students with special needs. Some researchers have experimented with elementary-level urban schools by introducing a "Good Behavior" game. Teachers were directed to identify acceptable and unacceptable behaviors clearly to their students. Then they were to observe the students during specified periods of time and count the numbers of unacceptable behaviors. The individual student or group of students receiving the smallest number of recorded unacceptable behaviors would win the game. The researchers found that using this technique both increased on-task behaviors and decreased disruptive behaviors in the students. This approach is considered to be generalizable to schools in nonurban settings.

Factors in school that influence students' motivation to learn

One factor that is found to increase students' motivation to learn is a sense of belonging in their school settings and a sense of having caring relationships. This includes the students' feeling that their families and friends support them and their education, and in school particularly, that their teachers are supportive. Individualizing and personalizing their instruction is one way that teachers accomplish this. Teachers also create caring, supportive social environments in school by demonstrating interest in their students' lives, inside and outside school. Students experiencing such positive interpersonal relationships are found to display more positive attitudes and values regarding school, and more satisfaction with it, and to attend school more, learn more, and report more academic engagement. Another factor is clearly defined, high, consistent, and realistically attainable teacher expectations of student performance. A third factor promoting students' cognitive engagement is teachers' use of active pedagogical strategies challenging students to tackle new ideas, explain their thinking, defend their decisions, and/or explore alternate methods and solutions, especially through peer collaboration.

Student activities that promote student engagement

Educational research has found that students are more likely to experience and demonstrate greater classroom engagement over the long term of their education when teachers assign them to such hands-on, authentic activities as constructing models; planning, implementing, completing, and reporting on projects; participating in role-play exercises; participating in debates on topics relevant to school subjects and activities; and planning and conducting experiments, making conclusions about them, and reporting their results to their classmates and teachers. Studies have also shown that teachers can make the lessons that they teach more relevant and meaningful to students when these lessons draw from and build upon the students' existing background knowledge, cultural backgrounds, and experiences in the real world and life. When the material that they study is personally interesting to students and related to their lives, they both learn more effectively and also enjoy the learning process more.

Establishing rapport in early elementary grades

Teachers report warm lighting helps create a cozy, "at-home" atmosphere. Many elementary teachers assign a theme for the school year, like bugs, birds, fish, or rocks. They display posters illustrating the theme, including catchphrases expressing their learning strategies; incorporate the theme in first-day handouts, student folders, and parent letters; devise activities around the theme, like reading books to the class about the theme and assigning student pairs/small groups to design an original bug. On first days, teachers assign activities enabling students to move around, become comfortable with the classroom, get acquainted with each other, work collaboratively, and think creatively. They use games—searching for all classmates' names in puzzles or physically finding each classmate and collecting their signatures. Teachers use "brainteasers" to engage students in creative problem-solving. They take inventories of student interests on first days. And they assign students artistic activities—like cutting out and illustrating paper "T-shirts" identifying their preferences, interests, future dreams, past experiences, and adjectives describing themselves.

Modeling to teach eye contact, vocal tone, and pronunciation

Many autistic students avoid eye contact, as do some cognitively impaired students and even nondisabled younger students. Often they do not understand its importance and have no practice using it. Some teachers with teaching assistants or aides find it helps to model through conversations with them: the teacher says to the assistant that s/he noticed how the assistant's eyes were looking right at a student's eyes when they were talking; that this showed the student the assistant was listening, and the assistant could see the student was also listening; and praises the assistant for "good eye contact." The assistant replies that good eye contact during conversation is good manners. The same technique can be used to describe appropriate vocal tones for conversations and correct pronunciation. The teacher can follow up by asking students to demonstrate good eye contact when greeting another student. They observe and provide prompts as needed. This is most effective when the teacher immediately rewards the interaction with verbal praise, plus applause from the class.

Successfully relating to and instructing high school students

Experienced high school teachers find that classroom success centers on three crucial areas: establishing rapport with the students; setting the teacher's rules and expectations for the class; and having strategies to promote students' motivation to learn. While teacher education students and new teachers observing experienced teachers may feel they seem to do it by some kind of magic, the experienced teachers say that strategic planning is actually at the heart of establishing a rapport and developing good working relationships with their students. For example, a high school teacher can help to build rapport with a new class of students by presenting oneself as having a "stern yet caring" (as one teacher puts it) presence; set class rules and conduct other activities together *with* the students rather than unilaterally, which helps to establish a classroom community; and communicating one's expectations to the students clearly on the very first day of school.

Engaging disabled and younger students in paying attention to directions

Some experienced teachers use techniques like rhythmic clapping and/or chanting to engage student attention. For example, the teacher demonstrates a loud, rhythmic hand clap and tells the students that when they hear the teacher do this, they should stop what they are doing and imitate the hand clap. The teacher tells the students the clap means s/he has something important to share with them and to copy clapping when the teacher's hands go down, and s/he will know they are done when they make eye contact ("I see you looking at my eyes"). Teachers can chant directions, like "If you hear me, put your hands on your shoulders....If you hear me, put your hands on your hips....If you me, put your hands on your tummy...." Teachers enhance students' attention by modulating their voices. For students who do not pay attention, teachers instruct them aloud to be sure their hands are empty and they are looking at the teacher's eyes. Teachers may need to wait for all students to focus.

Establishing rapport with sixth-grade students

One way a sixth-grade teacher can get acquainted with new students is to give them surveys about their interests and surveys of Gardner's Multiple Intelligences to get ideas of students' preferences, strengths, needs, and learning styles. To assess student writing abilities and styles, a pre-assessment can involve writing a letter to the teacher about themselves. The teacher gives no pre-instructions on the steps of writing to discern what they already know how to do independently. The teacher may use her/his district's model for assessing writing. As icebreakers, teachers can assign as homework writing and illustrating a "Me" page, guided by teacher-given questions. They can have each student create a poster using the letters in their first name, filling the page with large "bubble" letters, and filling each letter with information, photos, or drawings about themselves. Then the teacher can display these in the classroom, integrating technology by adding printed digital photos of students to their posters. They can have students create PowerPoints and revise them at the end of the school year to add what they have learned.

Class rules for disabled and nondisabled high school students

The high school teacher can first establish basic, vital "ground rules" based on what the teacher needs in the classroom. For example, students must arrive on time and be prepared; respect both classmates and classroom materials; and follow directions the first time the teacher gives them. After conveying these rules, the teacher can involve students in collaborating to create class rules. This helps build a class community. The teacher can integrate the opinions and viewpoints of students by asking them simple questions, like why they are there and what they need to achieve their goals. The teacher records student answers, incorporating these in expanding on the ground rules. Involving students gives them a sense of a democratic class community instead of a dictatorship and stimulates processes of critical thinking. Teachers should also give students lists of daily materials needed and examples of acceptable versus unacceptable work, and inform students how they will assess their work (rubrics, etc.). Teachers should communicate their expectations orally, in print/writing, and visually.

Motivating high school students to read

Some high school teachers experienced in teaching teens who struggle with reading meet such challenges by getting students excited about reading. They find books their students can relate to and enjoy, and they can begin the school year by reading these books aloud to students. Only after they have stimulated student enjoyment and enthusiasm for reading do they assess students' current reading levels, using instruments like the Scholastic Reading Inventory. Teachers can use a Book Pass activity to help students become familiar with books in their class library and select books with topics interesting to them at suitable levels for independent reading. Small groups (like five each) designate one student timekeeper. Seated in circles, each group member previews the front and back of the book and begins reading that book. The timekeeper announces when 2 to 3 minutes elapse; students write down the book title, pages read, comments, and whether they would like reading it further. Students then pass the books to their right, repeating with another book. They finish with group sharing of individual book comments.

Safe, supportive, and positive elementary classroom and school climate

Elementary school teachers realize that students will be more engaged in school and learning if it is fun and they are happy. Some teachers help students consolidate what they just learned and/or take a break from schoolwork with a group singing period in the classroom. A few weeks into the school year, once students have gotten to know each other and developed into a cohesive group, some teachers have them vote for an alliterative class name reflecting their interests, ambitions, and/or attitudes. The teacher calls them by this group name when they are lining up to leave the room and at other key moments to reinforce their feelings of belonging and ownership. To encourage and reinforce student responsibility, some elementary teachers assign a job to each student for the week, posting these on a chart on the wall, and all of the students take turns assuming different weekly job rotations.

Communicating expectations of students and regular routines

Some schools use an acronym like BEST, representing Be respectful, Enjoy learning, Stay safe, and Totally responsible, to help students remember these principles. Some teachers have students negotiate their classroom expectations, keeping them generally consistent with school expectations, and on reaching consensus, they display pictures and words on the walls reflecting these. They also discuss choices and how expectations keep everyone safe. They set routines, posting their daily schedule on the wall and discussing it. Some teachers institute weekly lessons involving behavioral tasks explicitly teaching behavioral expectations aligned with school values, and they post these on the wall. Some teachers use a token economy. For example, each student gets a smiley face on a chart for making good choices; upon accumulating 10, the student can select a prize, which the teacher reports schoolwide to record all recognition of positive behaviors. When students do not meet expectations, some teachers explicitly model and teach expected behavior, like teaching how to apologize sincerely for hitting/kicking, with the victim choosing whether to accept the apology.

Addressing and preventing bullying

In April 2013, the U.S. Department of Justice arrived at a settlement agreement with the Metropolitan School District of Decatur Township, Indiana. This concluded a review of district practices and policies regarding bullying and harassment, prompted by 2011 reports of possible racial targeting at one school. The district arranged to collaborate with the federally funded Great Lakes Equity Center at Indiana University-Purdue University Indianapolis on actions against bullying for disability, race, national origin, color, gender, or religion and promoting safe, supportive learning environments for all students. Actions include creating a district-wide antiharassment task force to review and revise district harassment/bullying and disciplinary policy and procedures; creating a coherent process to receive, investigate, and monitor bullying/harassment complaints, and track repeating instances involving groups/individuals in special classes; and give students and staff at two district schools school climate assessments, training, and professional development. A Civil Rights Division spokesperson said these affirmative steps provide statewide and nationwide examples. Nationwide work against school bullying also aligns with federal civil rights legislation.

Icebreakers to use to get acquainted with high school students

Experienced high school teachers find adolescents are primarily concerned with adjusting to the new setting and getting acquainted with new classmates, and teachers need to start the year by familiarizing themselves well with new students. To help both teacher and students get acquainted, teachers can use icebreaker activities. One involves "matching" index cards based on common interests of the school's student body. For example, teachers make card pairs like Bill Gates and Microsoft; Russell Simmons and Def Jam Records, etc. Each student gets one card and finds the student with a matching card. Then they interview each other. Teachers can suggest questions, like the last school they attended, their favorite book genre, pet peeves, favorite things, embarrassing incidents, hobbies, etc. Following interviews, each student presents information about his/her "match" to the class. Another activity groups and numbers students in fours; each student writes down adjectives describing themselves and alliterative with their names (e.g., "Shy Shannon" or "Bookish Brad"), and take turns introducing themselves and another student using these.

Integrating technology to motivate learning

To prepare and motivate adolescents to learn right away, high school teachers can integrate technology, yet need no more than a video camera and books when they assign projects the first week of school. For example, the teacher can ask the students to choose a book they have recently read and/or is their favorite. The teacher can lead a class discussion about characteristics in TV commercials that make the viewer remember the commercials best, like musical jingles; vivid visual imagery; strong slogans or tag lines; or humorous/incongruous situations. The teacher creates a model for students with a sample commercial. The teacher can then have the students make their own commercials advertising their chosen books. Another example of a project is to assign students to make their autobiographies, using videos about five minutes long. The teacher can guide the students to incorporate details related to their early childhoods; pets, friends, their home lives; their hobbies, what things interest them most, and what their major goals in life are.

Promoting parental support for children's education

Some teachers implement a practice of using a communication book for each student. These books are sent back and forth between the school and the students' homes for the teacher and parents to write correspondence to one another. Before calling the roll every morning, the teacher checks the communication books for new entries. (This practice likely works best with smaller class sizes.) Some elementary school teachers also invite all students' parents to visit their classrooms in the morning to help by reading or telling stories to the children to get them settled down and ready for the day. Some elementary school teachers regularly send notes to parents with students. For example, one teacher noticed her young students became hungry at midmorning, and the class agreed to schedule a snack period. She sent parents notes asking them to send healthy snack foods, including a list of appropriate, easy-to-prepare snacks. This teacher reported their snack time soon ran smoothly, with children usually eating and doing schoolwork concurrently.

Physical education for disabled students

Federal laws
The IDEA and other federal legislation for students with disabilities mandate that these students be provided physical education. Federal law defines physical education as the development of physical and motor skills; fundamental motor skills and patterns like catching, throwing, walking, running, etc.; and skills in individual and group sports, including intramural and lifetime sports, and in dance and aquatics. The IDEA mandates instruction in the least restrictive environment (LRE) possible. Regarding PE, this involves adaptations and/or modifications to curriculum and/or instruction as it does regarding academic education. In PE, adaptations/modifications assure each student's success in a safe environment. A student's IEP defines placement, which can include one or several options among the general physical education setting alone; this setting but with aid from teaching assistants or peers; a separate PE class setting with peers; a separate PE class setting with assistants; and/or settings with 1:1 student-instructor activities.

Potential modifications to games
To level the competition, PE teachers can modify activities. They can let special-needs students hit or kick instead of pitching a ball. In volleyball games, they can let students catch and throw the ball and/or let it bounce. Teachers can permit longer time periods equal to student ability for moving to a goal/base. When possible, they can schedule games inside the gym on smooth floors to facilitate movement instead of outdoors in a field. When modifying rules for disabled students, teachers can involve them in the decision-making process. Teachers can reduce distances by moving bases closer together; letting students get closer to the net/goal/target; and letting them serve from midcourt in volleyball/badminton/tennis. Teachers can provide more scoring opportunities by substituting four for three strikes/ten arrows for six/three for two foul shots/etc. They can assign disabled students to be pitchers/goalies/first basemen, or other positions requiring

less mobility. Adaptive equipment they can provide includes bigger bats/racquets; bigger/lighter/softer balls; and bigger baskets/goals/bases.

Benefits of inclusive educational programs

Educational research has found that both students with disabilities and their nondisabled peers obtain significant benefits from inclusive educational programs. For example, students with disabilities experience more stimulating learning environments via inclusion. They benefit from nondisabled role models of adaptive, communication, and social skills and behaviors. They have more opportunities for making new friends and sharing new experiences with them. They gain greater peer acceptance from being included, and they have a greater sense of membership in a regular class and in the school. Students without disabilities benefit by learning greater acceptance of individual differences among people. They learn to feel more comfort around students with various disabilities. They learn to help their disabled peers, which generalizes to learning to be more helpful to others. They gain leadership skills by providing examples, help, and guidance. And they gain greater self-esteem through modeling helpful leadership behaviors. Thus, inclusive education benefits all students.

Adapting the physical environment to facilitate learning

For students whose cognitive levels, attention spans, or other differences make large assignments intimidating, teachers can divide these into small, more achievable "chunks" so they are more willing to tackle them and experience some success daily. For students having difficulty taking notes from the blackboard, teachers can offer paper handouts/notes. Distractible students can be seated away from windows, noisy, high-traffic areas, and classmates who encourage chatting. Teachers must implement all adaptations in student IEPs, monitor their effectiveness, and discuss changes with the team if adaptations are not enabling best student performance. With students needing constant reminding of how to follow class practices, teachers can make an enlarged checklist of expectations for their daily assignments/routines and tape it to their binder/desktop, enabling more independent work tracking. Scheduling morning periods daily to check student homework and planners clarifies expectations and allows time to resolve problems and still have productive days. Assignments and assessments can use computers/scribes/time extensions/oral responses as alternatives for students with writing/printing difficulties.

Arranging physical space to accommodate students

Teachers must consider all learning community members' needs, including students, teachers, specialists, paraprofessionals, and volunteers. When community members change, last year's arrangement may not work. Teachers must also consider size and layout of their classroom/space, including attached equipment/furnishings, classroom location in the school, and instructional materials. Depending on curriculum and teaching philosophy and approach, teachers may want to arrange space for large and small groups, teams, cooperative learning groups, and individual instruction. If any student(s) use wheelchairs, teachers must consider accommodating their maneuvering in the room. They must consider preventing distractions for ADHD students. They may lower chalkboards, bulletin boards, and pencil sharpeners, and add bathroom grab bars for wheelchair students, and they may procure more electrical outlets for computers, language masters, and tape recorders for students with LDs or visual impairment. They may place carpet in areas for students needing to sit/lie on the floor periodically. Insurmountable obstacles may dictate extensive remodeling or relocation to different classrooms. Advance planning is hence necessary to allow budgeting and work without interrupting school-year instruction.

Teachers should allocate areas within their classroom for individualized teaching, and also small and large groups. The teacher and/or learning specialist might need a small-group instruction space. Teaching stations, learning centers, and areas for partner/pair work are good whenever possible. Teachers need to separate/designate noisy and quiet areas, and spaces free of distractions. According to educational research, horizontal and vertical paths must allow teachers to reach any student within eight steps. Wheelchairs require at least 36" to maneuver. Student coats and backpacks must be placed to avoid blocking traffic. Some experts suggest having students turn their desks so the lids open away from them, to keep them from accumulating unwanted/forgotten things inside. If a classroom faces the playground, a busy road, student cafeteria lines, and/or steady streams of traffic— especially since classroom relocation, even when available, can take extreme effort and a whole year—teachers can adapt existing spaces by putting curtains over windows, closing the door, and hanging visual displays from the ceiling that absorb sound.

Instructional accommodations and modifications

Accommodations are changes in HOW students learn and are assessed, while modifications are changes in WHAT students are expected to learn. Accommodations can involve teaching methods, materials, assignments, tests, the learning environment, scheduling, time demands, and special communications systems, and they need not change school learning goals. Modifications can involve partial program or course completion; lower than grade-level curriculum expectations; alternative curriculum goals; and alternate assessments. The IDEA mandates that schools give students with disabilities the chance to be included and progress in the general education curriculum, which can require accommodations and/or modifications to accomplish. The IDEA also requires all students receiving special education and related services to have IEPs Section 504 of the Rehabilitation Act that requires that schools provide accommodations to students with disabilities even if they do not have IEPs. The Americans with Disabilities Act (ADA) bans discrimination against the disabled. State laws follow the federal laws in allowing accommodations and modifications for students with disabilities.

Effective use of common spaces

While teachers have little or no control over their school building's commonly shared spaces, they can instruct their students to work with these. For example, they can teach them the common courtesies of walking quietly on the right side of the hall, and of speaking quietly in the library and cafeteria, auditorium, or cafeteria. This will help students adjust to large spaces inside the building. Teachers can also instruct all students to allow sufficient space for students using wheelchairs to go around corners and not to crowd wheelchairs. This not only helps the students in wheelchairs; it also prevents ambulatory students from being injured by coming too close to wheelchairs. Students in both special and general education programs must be taught to take special care in adhering to rules and guidelines on the playground and in the school gymnasium. Students make successful adaptations to school building spaces when they have learned how to navigate from one place to another, and how to behave in each school area.

Accommodations for students with difficulties with self-control

Some students with disabilities can require alterations in the learning environment to assist them in managing their behavior. For some, behavior management plans and/or counseling services may be required. There are also classroom accommodations educators can make for students whether or not they have such behavior management plans and/or counseling services. For example, teachers can let students use study carrels or other enclosures to work independently with less distraction. Teachers can assign work that students are able to finish in shorter time durations. Teachers can also allow students to use timers to help them monitor how much more time they have to finish assignments and how much more time they need to complete their work. For students needing structure to promote behavioral self-control, teachers can positively reinforce following classroom rules, list consequences for breaking rules, and ensure students' knowledge of rules and consequences.

In addition to posting lists of classroom rules and consequences for breaking them and making sure all students know these, teachers can also make sure to supply students with activities to pursue during free time periods. Students requiring structure are apt to act out during unassigned times without the direction of something specific to do. To prepare students for transitions such as beginning new lessons, going to lunch, moving to other school areas, or changing classes, teachers should follow regular routines and give students prompts about the changes. Teachers may seat some students next to trained peers, teacher's aides, or volunteers to help them attend to lessons. They can also designate "study buddies" who know how to interact effectively with some students to help them when the teacher is otherwise occupied. For pupils who lack behavioral self-control without personal support and attention, the teacher can also conduct 1:1 instruction with certain students and work with others in small groups to address their needs.

Crisis intervention and prevention

In immediate responses to crises in schools, educators should concentrate on restoring equilibrium for students. Their demeanor should be calm, authoritative, and nurturing; their behaviors direct, informative, and oriented to problem-solving. Educators should address student denial by providing them with accurate information and realistic explanations about what happened and what they can expect. Reassurance should never be untrue or unrealistic. Educators should encourage students to face the factual aspects of a crisis. They should invite students to cope with their emotional responses, and discuss with them their responses and defense mechanisms. They should communicate to students a sense of positive expectations and hope, in that although crises bring changes, they have means of coping with these. Educators can shift students' positions from victims to actors by helping them plan appropriate, realistic, and salutary actions to follow after they separate, building upon demonstrated student coping skills and techniques, and when appropriate, engage them in helping restore equilibrium. They should link students with peers, family, and staff for immediate social support.

Three main elements of responding to and preventing crises in schools are: Communication; Direction and Coordination; and Health and Safety. During a crisis, educators communicate: they sound alarms if needed; clarify next steps; give information about the occurrence and first-aid station locations, etc.; control rumors about the event; interact with the media as needed, and with the school district and community; respond to parent concerns; and keep

- 42 -

track of the students and staff. Direction and coordination during a crisis include monitoring and solving problems and directing emergency operations centers. Health and safety during the emergency include directing evacuation, security, search and rescue operations; providing first aid for medical and psychological injuries; and reducing hazards to students and staff. Immediately after a crisis, communication includes dispelling rumors, clarifying crisis sources and impacts, and supplying information on medical and psychological resources available. Direction and coordination include continuing problem monitoring and solving. Health and safety include continuing activities begun during the crisis.

In the days and/or weeks following a school crisis, educators continue communication by supplying information and counseling to promote closure to students, school personnel, parents, and other school district and community members. They continue direction and coordination by monitoring and solving problems ensuing from the crisis. They continue health and safety by supplying case management, direct services, and/or referral for longer term treatments as needed to those involved. In efforts to prevent future crises, educators demonstrate communication by conducting debriefing meetings with school staff, parents, other community members, district personnel, and students as appropriate to make clear any deficits in their response to the recent crisis. They demonstrate direction and coordination by applying debriefing analysis to plan possible prevention of additional crises; limit the impacts of inevitable occurrences; and improve crisis response procedures and resources. They provide health and safety education to students, parents, and staff.

Difficulties in reading and following instructional methods

Many students with various disabilities have difficulties in the classroom due to problems they experience with following the instructional methods and reading and applying the textbooks and other printed or written learning materials used in regular education programs. Educators can help these students to work around such difficulties by providing them with accommodations. One of the most important skills to enable success in school is being able to read. However, many students who have disabilities are not reading at their grade level because of various impediments to their reading skills. Some are still in the process of acquiring fundamental skills in phonics (i.e., the relationship between speech sounds and the alphabetic letters that represent them) and word recognition. Some students are still in the process of learning how to apply techniques to assist them in comprehension of printed words, phrases, and sentences. In addition, plenty of textbooks, worksheets, and similar learning materials are not well-organized or clearly articulated, constituting further challenges to these students.

Accommodations for students with trouble understanding oral presentations

Some students with disabilities have trouble deciphering what they are meant to learn from an oral lecture or discussion on an academic topic. Teachers can make such accommodations as visual aids, like supporting their oral presentations with overhead projectors, large charts, or blackboards. They can give students an overview of a lesson's content before presenting it, and also introduce students to new vocabulary words prior to the lesson. Immediately following an oral lesson or lecture, teachers can give a printed summary of its important points, accompanied by a list of questions for them to answer. To help students with difficulties following ideas in oral lectures and discussions, teachers can break up lectures with discussions or other activities in small groups, and also maintain

- 43 -

student engagement by inviting their questions. They can identify the primary parts of steps in the information. They can write important ideas on chalkboards/whiteboards, emphasizing parts using different colors.

When students with various disabilities have trouble with taking notes on the teacher's oral lectures or lessons, the teacher can distribute printed copies of their lecture notes to accompany the oral presentation. They can allow these students to record orally presented class lessons, lectures, and discussions for their review and study. Teachers should repeat important concepts, paraphrase them to express them in more than one set of words, and provide students with summaries of all the most important points. It is especially helpful if teachers repeat, paraphrase, and summarize at the end of a lesson, lecture, or class discussion. Teachers can help students with taking notes by giving them copies of their overhead projector documents, diagrams, and/or outlines of their lectures. To reinforce the information in oral presentations, teachers should supplement them with charts, diagrams, written/printed text, and/or pictures, and repeat as frequently as needed. Also, for deaf or hard-of-hearing students, teachers should procure a sign-language interpreter or a note-taker.

Accommodations for students with trouble learning math

Some students who have various disabilities have deficient skills in basic arithmetic and may still depend on counting on their fingers beyond the usual age. Some students with disabilities have major problems with remembering fundamental facts related to math. For students who have trouble with understanding mathematical concepts and solving math problems, teachers can provide accommodations such as giving them concrete objects and materials to assist in learning math concepts. Many students who cannot understand abstract ideas solely through mental processes can succeed better when they can process them using concrete, tangible things they can see, touch, and manipulate. Teachers can also highlight or color-code the important words in mathematical word problems for students. They can allow students to utilize charts to plan how they will solve math problems. And they can permit students to use basic fact charts and/or calculators to follow formulas and compute numbers for solving math problems.

Accommodations for students with trouble reading

One common problem for students with disabilities is isolating the main ideas in a book they are reading and/or which parts are important to remember. Teachers can highlight the important concepts and instruct students to read these first. They can give study guides to students for independent reading. They can offer students books on the same subjects at lower grade levels to make the main ideas easier to identify. Some students comprehend information when they hear it, but cannot read it. Teachers can supply books on tape/recorded versions; videos or movies of the information; computer text-to-speech software programs; and/or assign classmates to read printed materials aloud to students. Students with blindness or visual impairments may need specially produced materials and/or equipment to access class information. Teachers can supply books on tape or texts with large print; books and other materials in Braille or embossed formats; and give students equipment like magnifying devices or optical enhancers.

Accommodations for students who have trouble with handwriting

Students with a number of different disabilities can have difficulty with the fine motor control involved in handwriting. In general, the same kinds of classroom accommodations are required to address disabled student needs for both written assignments and written tests. For example, if a student needs to complete a written assignment using a word processor, s/he will also need the word processor to complete a written test. For students having difficulties with fine motor control, teachers can allow them to write straight into their workbooks instead of on separate paper or on photocopies of the workbook pages. They can permit students to type on typewriters, word processors, or computer keyboards. They can arrange for students to dictate their assignment and/or test responses to scribes, like classmates or teaching assistants, who write down their dictations. Teachers can also allow and provide adaptive equipment for students, such as special pen/pencil holders or grips, pens with erasable ink, and special paper featuring raised/embossed lines or color-coded line ruling.

Accommodations for students who have trouble with expressive language

Many students with disabilities may have good ideas, but have difficulties with expressing these in writing and/or speech. Teachers can provide them with accommodations that can facilitate their use of expressive language. For example, they can allow students to use a thesaurus to look up words that express the ideas they want to convey, and to find additional synonyms and antonyms for words if their actual vocabularies and/or their access to retrieving words they know are limited. Teachers can allow and provide to students specialized word-processing software programs that predict the words that students are trying to express. They can allow students to make use of electronic spelling aids and/or spelling dictionaries to support correct orthography. Teachers should also grade the content of written assignments separately from the writing mechanics in academic subjects (other than English composition, grammar, or spelling). They should additionally allow students with disabilities to correct their grammatical and spelling errors when they are completing written assignments or assessments.

Accommodations for students who have trouble completing assigned work

Some students with disabilities can do the same work as others, but much more slowly. This can cause them to run out of time to finish assignments. Other students have trouble remembering to assemble the materials and resources they will need to complete assignments. For students who have trouble keeping track of their class assignments, teachers can provide accommodations by dividing longer assignments into portions and giving students separate due dates for each portion. Teachers can instruct students to mark their assignments' due dates on a calendar they can see. To accommodate students who work more slowly than others, teachers can assign a smaller total amount of work, while still ensuring that the items or tasks they choose are those necessary for meeting all the learning objectives they have identified. Teachers can allow these students to use instructional materials and resources outside of class. Until students can complete assignments on time, teachers can provide them with reinforcement via partial credit for incomplete or late work.

Accommodations on tests

Five main categories wherein accommodations are permitted on standardized tests are presentation, response, schedule, setting, and assistive technology. Insofar as they are legally allowed on standardized tests, students with disabilities generally need the same kinds of accommodations for classroom and standardized assessments. Accommodations enable students to demonstrate their mastery of skills and knowledge without their disabilities interfering. For students with reading deficits, teachers can read test items aloud to them (excluding reading skills tests). They can supply text-to-speech software to present students with test directions and/or nonreading test items. They can let students read test items to themselves instead of presenting them orally. They can supply Braille or large-print test forms, and/or visual magnifiers, auditory amplifiers, or other assistive technology. To aid in focusing visually on tests, teachers can have students use positioning tools, pointers, blank cards, templates, colored, blank overlays, or transparencies. To decrease auditory distraction, they can give students headphones and "white noise" machines.

Accommodating students who have trouble following directions

In general, teachers speak, write, or demonstrate to students what they want them to do in school. Some students with disabilities have difficulty attending to spoken, written, or demonstrated information; some with remembering it; and some with both attending and retaining it. Moreover, some students with disabilities have difficulty comprehending and/or applying directions. When students find it hard to remember what they were instructed to do, teachers can provide accommodations by asking them to repeat the instructions in their own words or to demonstrate physically what they were instructed to do. They can also teach these students how to use personal planners or assignment notebooks for keeping track of assignments and tests. When students have difficulty comprehending the teacher's instructions, the teacher can provide accommodations by giving directions broken down into consecutive steps, and furnishing pictures or outlines of them. They can demonstrate for students how to complete sample tasks or problems, and combine oral instructions with pictures, diagrams, and/or printed words.

When students with disabilities are taking classroom and/or standardized tests, they can often have difficulty with accessing, understanding, and/or following the directions in the tests. Teachers can provide classroom accommodations to these students to facilitate test-taking. For example, they can provide answer forms or test forms with visual symbols, like stop signs, arrows, etc., to guide students in following directions. Some standardized tests already include such symbols for all students. When test directions are presented orally, teachers can provide sign language interpreters for deaf or hard-of-hearing students. When test directions and writing prompts are presented in print, teachers can read these aloud for students with visual impairments, cognitive disabilities, and reading-related learning disabilities. For students who need it, teachers can reread test directions or further explain their meaning. Teachers can also highlight or underline the most important words in test directions and/or test items for students with disabilities.

Accommodating students who have problems with organization

Students with attention deficits, cognitive impairments, and other disabilities can be distracted more easily than usual, causing them to confuse or forget the teacher's instructions. Students who find it hard to pay attention to more than one thing at a time frequently encounter difficulty completing complex assignments. Compounding these, some instructional materials are unclear by nature, and materials with excessive details can cause disabled students great confusion. Additionally, many disabled students have trouble storing, finding, and keeping track of classroom materials. Teachers can provide accommodations for confusion with complexity in materials and instructions by color-coding different materials or tasks to help students identify them. They should arrange tasks in clear, uncluttered formats with obvious beginning points and step sequences. To help students keep their materials organized, teachers can provide them with special binders or folders with dividers and different colors for each subject and unit. Teachers can also provide students with checklists of the materials they need for each class, which students keep in/on their binders, desks, or lockers.

Accommodations for students who have difficulty understanding test directions

When students with disabilities are not sure what to do on tests, teachers should avoid hinting at right/wrong answers but still accommodate them verbally by encouraging them (e.g., to answer each question and continue working), and they should give them additional examples of test items for practice to ensure they know what to do during actual testing. Most standardized tests prohibit accommodations in presentation that alter the assessed skill; for example, if a test measures reading skills, teachers cannot read items aloud to students. However, certain accommodations are permissible for classroom assessments. For students having difficulty switching among task types, teachers can group similar items and place easiest items first on tests. They can divide matching tasks into smaller groups of 4 to 5 items each. For essay/fill-in-the-blank items, they can provide applicable word lists. Whenever memorization is not required, teachers can let students take open-book tests. On multiple-choice tests, teachers can remove one choice from each question. Teachers can select test questions covering all content required but give fewer total questions.

Accommodations for students who have trouble sustaining attention on tests

When administering state standardized tests, teachers may provide some accommodations to disabled students who struggle to maintain their attention and energy during testing. For example, teachers may monitor student answer sheets to see whether they are putting their responses in the right places. When student responses to extended-response items are partly correct, teachers may give partial credit as designated by the rubrics for these items on state standardized achievement tests. In classroom assessments, teachers may furnish students with prepared outlines, charts, diagrams, and/or webs to help them plan essay or open-ended question responses. Students may demonstrate their skills and knowledge via alternate formats like role-plays, oral interviews, or physical demonstrations. They may be allowed references like thesauruses, dictionaries, or almanacs. They may be allowed concrete manipulatives to do and/or check calculations. Students may retake tests and get credit for improving. Also, some state standardized tests even allow certain grades to retake them.

Accommodations students may need regarding location of test

Some students with special needs are so easily distracted that they cannot perform to their ability if they take a test in a large group. Accommodations to address this problem include administering the test to the student in isolation or in a smaller group; allowing the student to take the test in a study carrel or other enclosure; or having the student take the test in another room free of distractions. Other students have physical or sensory disabilities that have an impact on their ability to take a test. In such cases, schools and teachers need to allow these students to use whatever adaptive equipment or furniture they require to be able to participate in the assessment. One important consideration in allowing the use of assistive technology is that it does not alter the performance of the actual skills being tested. For example, if a test measures skills in reading printed language, a student could not use text-to-speech software for that particular test.

Accommodations students may need for providing test answers

Students with various disabilities can have difficulty handwriting test answers, circling or checking multiple-choice answers, filling in bubbles, or solving problems and explaining their solutions. Accommodations often allowed on standardized tests in some states include giving additional space for students to handwrite their answers; allowing students to answer questions orally instead of in writing, to dictate their answers into a sound recorder, or to a scribe or test proctor; or allowing the student to sign his or her test responses to a sign-language interpreter. Students may also be permitted to use word processors or computer or typewriter keyboards to answer test questions, although state standardized tests typically prohibit their using spell-check and grammar-check software when typing. Students may write into their test booklets instead of on separate sheets, create Braille answers on separate paper, or record their answers using speech-to-text software programs. Students are also often allowed to use outlines, charts, and/or diagrams for planning essay or open-ended question responses on tests.

Assistive technology

Students with various disabilities may need assistive technology to acquire the information they are expected to learn and/or to communicate what they have learned. As long as the purpose of assessment is not defeated, the skills being assessed are not changed, and the student's responses still reflect his or her independent efforts, students can generally use the same assistive technology they use during classroom instruction to complete assessments. For example, a student with a disability might be given an accommodation allowing him or her to use an adaptive calculator for solving mathematics problems on a test. Some state standardized achievement tests allow students in seventh through tenth grades, for example, to use calculators. Another example involves completing answers to essay questions and/or long explanations or answers to questions on tests. Students with disabilities may be permitted to use assistive technology, such as voice recorders to dictate their responses, or word processors to type them.

Accommodations regarding test schedule

Some students with disabilities need additional time to finish taking a test. Students who work very slowly, those who can work for only briefer periods at a time, and those using certain types of assistive technology may need alterations in testing schedules. Accommodations when administering typical state standardized tests include allowing longer times for students to take the test; dividing a test into smaller portions and allowing students to take each portion on a different day if necessary; permitting students to take short breaks during the testing period; and allowing students to take a test at different times of day if physical conditions and/or medications affect their alertness and attention. Teachers may provide additional accommodations not allowed on standardized tests for classroom assessments. For example, the teacher can give disabled students fewer test questions, as long as they still cover all the same skills and content being assessed. Teachers may also let students review and correct their test answers from the day before.

Unusual or unique test accommodations required by some students

Some students can have disabilities that necessitate more unusual accommodations in order to participate in state standardized achievement testing. Testing accommodations identified as unique usually entail some changes in the existing assessment materials. Typically, states will allow such unique assessment accommodations if their Commissioner of Education has previously approved their use. Parents and teachers can look to the program of educational services to exceptional students in their school district to assist them with making a request for approval of such accommodations. Several examples of unique or unusual accommodations that may be approved for students with disabilities to participate in standardized assessments include: test forms with fewer items on each page; test forms with more space separating each item from the next; test forms with modified or tabbed pages to enable students to turn pages more easily; and having test question and response forms attached to the student's work area to prevent their falling, sliding, or shifting to facilitate reading and writing or marking on them.

Adapting class schedules and time constraints

Many students with disabilities learn and/or work at slower speeds than their nondisabled peers. Others perform better without the pressure of rigorous schedules. Teachers can provide them with time- and schedule-related accommodations. For example, some high school students may be given an Incomplete course grade and finish the course in summer school or the next semester. On practice assignments with multiple similar items, students who have the cognitive ability to learn without excessive repetition but need additional time and/or perform poorly under time pressure may be permitted to complete only every other item. Another educator consideration regarding students with disabilities is that in middle school and high school programs, it is particularly critical to assign these students to classes appropriate for them. Teachers of special education are advised that they may facilitate this process by working with their school administrators to ensure that the schedules of assigned classes are able to accommodate the special needs of any students who have disabilities.

Some students who have disabilities can handle the same course content as their peers, but they need more time to do so, or they need their work to be broken up into shorter time periods with breaks in between. Some students with disabilities suffer deterioration in their performance when they feel pressured by time limits. Some also require more time to complete assignments and assessments due to the adaptive equipment they must use in order to participate. Some strategies teachers can use include keeping schedules flexible to allow students with disabilities more time to finish a course. This can include completing the requirements in summer school. Teachers can allow students with disabilities extra time to complete their classwork and take tests. They can assign work further in advance to allow students with disabilities a chance to begin their assignments earlier. Teachers can also supply students with clear schedules of all units, assignments, and tests, and include periodic checkpoints within these schedules to help students monitor their progress.

NIMAS

The IDEA incorporates the National Instructional Materials Accessibility Standard or NIMAS. The stated purpose of this standard is to "facilitate the provision of accessible, alternate-format versions of print textbooks to pre-K–12 students with disabilities." This standard provides information to assist school IEP teams in deciding how they can electronically provide access to textbooks and other reading materials to students who have dyslexia and other LDs with reading. Parents who have children with reading disabilities should look at their children's IEPs and/or 504 plans to discover whether they contain anything about eligibility for accessible instructional materials, or AIM. If a student was determined not to be eligible for AIM, parents have the legal right to talk with their school personnel about why not. Parents can advocate for their children with schools by initiating conversations about how their children learn best, and how alternative formats, digital software, and/or readers can sometimes strikingly improve their learning and their motivation and confidence in it.

AIM

AIM stands for Accessible Instructional Materials. Many students with disabilities find reading impossible or difficult because of various disabilities affecting being able to read standard printed materials. AIMs consist of textbooks and other printed educational materials published in special digital formats. These formats provide accommodation to individuals who are blind, visually impaired, have various physical disabilities, and have reading-related learning disabilities (LDs) including dyslexia. Using digital formats enables students with reading and/or print disabilities to hear and see the text simultaneously using a computer, tablet, or other digital device. AIM includes formats like Braille, large print, audio, and digital text. The standard format for digital text files is named DAISY, for Digital Accessible Information System. DAISY allows users to listen to recordings of human voices or electronic speech synthesizers for audio versions of print materials. Accompanying reading software presents text visually at the same time. Today, most young students are comfortable and familiar with electronic voices and adapt easily to using them for reading.

Resources providing accessible text formats

Two organizations whose specialty is providing accessible text formats are Bookshare at bookshare.org and Learning Ally at learningally.org. Bookshare is an online library of over 150,000 digital versions of copyrighted textbooks and other books. Learning Ally is an online library of more than 70,000 audio versions of literary works and textbooks, with both recordings of human voices and digitally synthesized voices reading the material. These organizations both have approval from the U.S. Department of Education for providing accessible instructional materials (AIM) to school districts and individual schools. Schools and/or districts can request digital formats or files from these groups for qualifying students with reading or print disabilities. Due to their cooperative missions, qualified members of either organization can more easily gain membership in the other. Some school districts or schools even pay for memberships in both organizations or either one for students who are found eligible.

Research evidence regarding text-to-speech technology

Studies suggest that reading technologies that use audio or digital formats can enhance the reading process for students with learning disabilities. When students simultaneously see words and sentences highlighted on the screens of computers, tablets, or other devices and hear them read aloud via text-to-speech (TTS) programs, this is described as "multisensory" or "multimodal" reading. With digital education widespread today, students may learn at home or while on the go as well as in the classroom. In this environment, AT programs are compatible with student learning processes. Some high-quality programs include Read Write Gold by TextHelp; Read: OutLoud by Don Johnston; and Kurzweil 3000 by Cambium. For iPads and other Apple devices, the large online digital library Bookshare offers an application ("app") called Read2Go, which enables its members to download and read its digital books on their devices. Students can digitally navigate through books' tables of contents, chapters, pages, and paragraphs.

Challenges in converting elements in print books to digital formats

According to the National Center for Learning Disabilities, certain visual images in printed books—for example, mathematical concepts, charts, and graphs—cannot be accurately represented using text-to-speech software programs. This presents a limitation to what students with reading or other disabilities can access compared to the original printed book versions. However, progress in technology is addressing this need. The organization Benetech is the parent group of the extensive online library known as Bookshare (bookshare.org). Benetech has a division called the DIAGRAM Center. At the DIAGRAM Center, designers of digital technology have created a new web application tool named POET. POET is an open-source application that enables crowd sourcing of verbal descriptions of visual images. In addition, it facilitates the process of creating descriptions of visual images for Digital Accessible Information System or DAISY file format, the standard format for digital text files. The progress of this and similar technology developments afford increased access to text for students with disabilities.

Research findings concerning instruction of literacy, math, and science

Comprehensive literature reviews find nearly twice as much research exists about teaching literacy as math, and four times more about math than science. One commonality among these areas is that using behavior analysis principles is effective for teaching them all to severely developmentally disabled students. For example, using task analysis to break down the instruction of multistep (chained) tasks and using time delay for teaching separate tasks are both highly effective for teaching academic content. These techniques are used in systematic instruction, which studies show is an effective overall teaching strategy for these students. Systematic instruction has been used to teach feeding, toileting, dressing, safety, and many other functional skills, and academic skills as well. Systematic instruction procedures define observable, measurable target skills; collect intervention data to prove new skill acquisition; apply behavioral principles and techniques like systematic prompts and fading, error correction, and differential reinforcement to aid transfer of learned skills; and effect behavioral changes that can be generalized across skills, materials, people, and contexts.

Digital books

Today, students can download and read books digitally on tablets, other devices, and computers from online digital libraries, which even offer apps (applications) for downloading to digital devices. Students can interact with, manipulate, and change settings in digital reading matter, including the sizes and colors of the fonts, both in the text and in hypertext links; choosing between male or female voices in audio versions of text; adjusting the speed of the readers' speech in audio text; turning on and off the read-aloud function in books with both visual and audio text; setting bookmarks in books; and changing the appearances of background displays in digital books. Some software programs and portable devices incorporate graphic organizers to aid comprehension and studying; note-taking tools to aid in essay writing; built-in scanners to copy and upload/download documents and pictures; support tools for outline writing; dictionaries, spell-checkers; keyword searches; bibliographers; voice recorders, voice recognition; and Acapela Voices, which reads text aloud translated into Spanish and other languages for ESL/ELL students.

Effective instruction in reading

According to the National Reading Panel, three main components of effective instruction in reading are (1) phonemic awareness, phonics, and alphabet knowledge; (2) vocabulary, text comprehension, and reading fluency; and (3) reading comprehension strategies. When the National Center for Learning Disabilities surveyed teachers and assistive technology (AT) specialists about digital technologies and digital books, the consensus of their responses identified a number of benefits. These included that digital reading technology affords a whole new world of learning potential for students, and that it affords flexibility among more learning options according to student preferences and learning styles. Teachers and AT specialists also find that digital reading options further the personal achievement, independence, and socialization skills of students. They say digital reading does much to aid students who struggle with decoding printed words. It keeps students' attention for longer time spans. It helps students read at their grade levels. It encourages students to take notes and make annotations to texts. And it corrects students' spelling errors.

Evidence-based strategies for teaching science

Recent educational research studies have shown that teachers, when trained in a specific task analysis, could teach developmentally disabled students to conduct science experiments. Some researchers have used graphic organizers to teach science core content to students with autism in middle school. Others taught science vocabulary and concepts to similar students using explicit instruction of descriptors. And some have taught the steps of scientific inquiry lessons, and science concepts that the learners generalized to new materials, to students with moderate intellectual disabilities. Research has shown that time delay and similar strategies for special educators to teach math and science vocabulary across multiple academic content areas is effective with high school students having moderate and severe developmental disabilities. Other researchers have recently investigated teaching early science concepts and vocabulary to elementary school students with severe DDs. They find even at lower ages/grades and more severe disabilities, students learned comprehension of both scientific vocabulary and concepts, meeting the criteria of state standards for progress through science lessons in the general education curriculum.

ESL classes

American classrooms where students are learning English as a new language demand much more interaction between students and teachers than other classrooms generally do. Many activities assigned in ESL classes involve group work, which necessitates moving desks, getting up, and moving around, which must be kept in mind for disabled students. Teachers should also be sensitive to the diversity of most ESL classes, which often include students from different countries and of various ages. ESL teachers can help by educating themselves in advance about any specific disabilities incoming students to their classes have. They should ensure their classes are inclusive, by providing accommodations and/or services needed by disabled students, and communicating this to students clearly in their course syllabi and in other ways. They should discuss with disabled students how their needs and accommodations might change, and any help or adjustments such changes could necessitate.

Approach to having disabled students in ESL classroom

ESL teachers with disabled students should discuss their needs and accommodations with the students. They should also discuss these with their teaching assistants, aides, school office staff, and other support staff, and also request that they help with accommodations for these students. Teachers must observe privacy regulations and not disclose disability information with faculty, staff, or other students, except in regard to accommodations that are needed. In the United States, the law requires schools, agencies, and other organizations to provide the same accommodations to international students with disabilities as they do to U.S. citizens; ESL teachers in America should comply with this legal requirement. All world nations have organizations that provide access to local resources for people with disabilities. ESL teachers with disabled students can contact these groups for resources and advice. Regardless of the type of disability, teachers should concentrate on the individual student's abilities and strengths.

Depending on the type and extent of a disability and the classroom situation, students with various disabilities can find everyday classroom activities difficult, e.g., active learning that involves getting up and engaging in different physical actions; making physical and oral presentations; or participating in group or class discussions. ESL teachers can exercise their creativity by adapting the activities they design and assign to allow more universal student access, while still attaining the same learning goals. When an ESL teacher has a student with a disability in the class, the teacher should communicate the same expectations and standards for academic achievement and personal behavior that s/he has for all students. The majority of students with disabilities appreciate being treated with the same educational standards and teacher expectations as a sign of respect from the teacher. ESL teachers should also ask their disabled students regularly for feedback about what things in class work and do not work for them, and how things that do not work may be adjusted or modified.

Communication skills and instruction for blind or visually impaired students

While teachers routinely use visual aids like pictures, flash cards, graphs, charts, and pointing at objects in the room while saying "this" or "that," they must realize these are not accessible to blind or visually impaired students. They must provide them with additional tactile versions and/or verbal descriptions. Students with low vision may not be able to see writing on blackboards/whiteboards, in workbooks, etc. They should be seated at the front of the room and allowed to bring their own magnifying devices. Before class, teachers can provide handouts to these students in Braille, large print, audio formats, or electronic formats depending on their preferred format, and/or give students additional prompts during class. When presenting visual information, teachers should spell new vocabulary words aloud; print using large, clear letters; use larger sized fonts in overheads and handouts; and read aloud as they write, which benefits all students. When drawing or displaying pictures, teachers should verbally describe their contents.

Equal access to classroom content for students with low vision or blindness

When school assignments involve large amounts of reading, students with low vision often experience eye fatigue and need to rest their eyes frequently. Teachers can permit them breaks during class and/or give them extensions on due dates for reading assignments. Teachers should ensure student access to alternative media formats like Braille, audio recordings, or large print. Some students bring laptops or other computerized devices with text-to-speech, large print, or Braille conversion software; teachers should provide their teaching content in electronic formats for these students. They should also discuss with them whether any websites the teacher uses as lesson supplements are incompatible with students' special software, and consider adjusting their curriculum to use compatible sites. Teachers should also keep classroom layout consistent to facilitate student orientation and navigation. Teachers sharing classrooms can try to enlist the other teachers' cooperation and assistance. Tactile and/or audio rather than visual cues more effectively get these students' attention. Teachers can also instruct other students to say their names before speaking during group discussions.

Considerations for students with mobility disabilities

When assigning group activities, teachers may need more flexibility and time for assembling groups and moving furniture. Teachers should consider this in assigning groups/pairs, without restricting variety among student partners/classmates. Students with limited/no use of their arms cannot perform common classroom behaviors like jotting down new vocabulary words, looking words up in dictionaries or encyclopedias, or even raising their hands. Teachers need to provide them with alternative methods, like a scribe to take notes, orally saying "yes"/"no" instead of raising hands, etc. Teachers can collaborate with students on alternative means to get teacher attention. Students in wheelchairs may arrive late and/or need to leave early because of weather, transportation service, architectural barriers, or other factors outside their control. Teachers should discuss with students whether their disability requiring accommodation or behavioral factors cause late arrivals/early departures, defining expectations and resolving issues accordingly. Teachers should ensure other students realize wheelchairs/other adaptive equipment constitute personal space and respect it. Teachers and students should sit when interacting with students of shorter stature or students in wheelchairs.

Instructional considerations for deaf and hard-of-hearing students

Some deaf/hard-of-hearing students learn written English and speech reading to understand hearing people, but communicate using sign language and do not learn speech. Others want to learn speech and have pronunciation difficulties due to their hearing loss. For students who want to use spoken English, teachers can find technological help. For example, microphones equipped with FM systems not only amplify speech sounds, but also send them directly to the student's hearing aids. Teachers can also repeat what other students say if they are out of microphone range, which benefits all students. For deaf students who communicate using sign language, teachers can engage the services of sign language interpreters; they can additionally learn several simpler signs themselves to facilitate basic communication with these students. Interpreting can be challenging for international students, because sign language is not universal but varies among countries. In this case, speech-to-text services may be better. Teachers should always directly address the student rather than the sign language interpreter/STT assistant.

Even deaf/HOH students who use spoken English are apt to have problems during class activities involving faster reaction times, like listen-and-repeat exercises. Teachers can give them more time to repeat, and also try to eliminate background noises—including cross-talk from other students—as possible. Fire alarms, other audio emergency signals, and PA speaker announcements are not usually accessible to deaf students. Teachers can accommodate them by flicking the overhead lights on and off, waving a hand, or touching them on the shoulder to get their attention before announcements or during alarms. Viewing videos of movies and TV programs is an activity often used and enjoyed in classrooms in general and even more so in ESL classes. However, teachers should be sure the videos include English closed captions or subtitles. This benefits comprehension for both deaf/HOH and ESL students. If captions/subtitles are unavailable for a video, teachers can procure sign language interpreters or speech-to-text note-takers. HOH students often comprehend video images better than audio practice.

Teachers should seek means of utilizing visual aids as supplements to all their lessons. They should wait to allow time for students to view both the signs of a sign language interpreter or the text of speech-to-text software programs, and also the visual aid the teacher presents. Teachers should be mindful whether they are standing between the student and interpreter. Teachers can also use color-coding, e.g., different pen colors to represent different parts of a sentence—like red for subjects or blue for verbs. They can use geometric shapes to adapt concepts visually and use their fingers to represent different subjects or different tenses when conjugating verbs. Since some deaf/hard-of-hearing students speech read, teachers should not stand in front of windows or other places that interfere with this. Seating in front of the room or circular seating wherein students can see both the teacher and classmates can help hearing-impaired students always see who is speaking. Decreasing background noise from open windows, large groups, fans, or cross-talk helps students follow class discussions.

Considerations for students with chronic health and mental health disabilities

Some students have different conditions like diabetes, asthma, seizure disorder, multiple sclerosis, arthritis, or anxiety, depression, obsessive-compulsive disorder, or bipolar disorder. Individual differences in symptoms complicate such chronic disabilities. Due to the condition, medication side effects, and/or the environment, students may feel/perform better/worse at certain times of the day/on certain days. This can influence attendance, attention, and memory. Teachers should permit students flexibility in taking breaks, extend time for finishing assignments, allow note-takers, adjust schedules, and let students make up missed tests as necessary. Some students with chronic conditions need rest at home for days/weeks, but may be able to study and do homework there. Teachers can design and adhere to a good syllabus to inform students what to do if they miss classes. Some students have sensitivities to sensory stimuli like temperature changes, lights, or sounds, or they have other conditions affecting classroom participation and/or social interactions. Teachers should make time to acquaint themselves with each student's unique circumstances and which accommodations help them most.

Teaching communication skills to students with speech disabilities

Some students have difficulty controlling their speech muscles secondary to cerebral palsy; some progressive illnesses cause speech problems; and traumatic brain injuries can cause aphasia, a language processing problem. Some students stutter, and some have voice disorders secondary to cleft palate/lip, vocal nodules/polyps, etc. Students who cannot speak functionally use electronic voice synthesizers or visual-manual communication boards/books. Others can speak, but less quickly, clearly and/or fluently than normal. Many students have milder articulation disorders that still affect their communication. Teachers not understanding a student should not say/pretend they do, but allow them to repeat; they are accustomed to it. Teachers should not finish their sentences for them, but give them time for self-expression, promoting self-confidence. Teachers must adjust their expectations for oral assignments/tests. They can also seek alternative means for students to attain class goals, e.g., hand-raising, writing, or group-texting question answers and slower discussion speeds. For students with communications assistants, teachers should address the student, not the assistant.

Teaching strategies for students with cognitive and learning disabilities

Students with learning and cognitive disabilities are increasingly common in today's classrooms and quite common in ESL classrooms where they can substantially affect how students learn English. Standard instructional methods for language are usually less effective for students with learning disabilities, autism spectrum disorders (ASDs), and various other neurological deficits. Teachers are responsible for modifying their teaching styles to facilitate learning, and ESL teachers to facilitate learning a new language. In ESL, students with LDs must not only process words and symbols; they also contend with various difficulties remembering/retrieving words, articulating speech sounds, fluency, organizing thoughts, constructing sentences, and thinking abstractly. Teachers should focus not on student deficits, but strategies many students have developed independently to compensate. Teachers can provide accommodations like more time for activities and tests; note-takers; and tutors. Neurological deficits that affect social skills, as with ASDs, can make group/pair activities challenging. Teachers should provide structure and lead classes deliberately, clarifying the goals and purposes of each segment of the class.

An ESL teacher may find that students with traumatic brain injuries or ADHD encounter difficulty in class, especially if the teacher presents information using only one format, modality, or approach. Teachers should use multimodal teaching approaches and alternative assessment formats. Utilizing a variety of instructional methods, e.g., lectures, games, small group assignments, or paired work, will make it easier for these students to find which technique(s) are most effective for them. Students with LDs often perform better in one modality and worse in another, e.g., excelling at spoken skills but struggling with written skills. Teachers can accommodate these students by offering them a variety of ways to demonstrate their learning, like doing assignments in artistic or oral formats. Teachers should also realize that individual differences give every student's neurological deficit a unique presentation, so they must discover solutions case by case. ESL teachers need to understand students' abilities/skills in their native languages to differentiate errors due to disabilities from those naturally due to learning a second language.

Self-confidence in disabled students

Many students with disabilities are aware of their disability, which can undermine their self-confidence. They often feel they are different and do not fit in socially and have experienced rejection, ridicule, and bullying by other students. Additionally, experiencing failure at tasks their nondisabled peers complete easily can lower their self-esteem. Teachers can offer explicit instruction, asking students to identify good qualities they possess; help them develop positive affirmations they can understand, repeat, and believe; and provide plentiful positive reinforcement for every small success and for admirable efforts regardless of outcome. They can have students describe how they think others see them, and collaborate to develop strategies to improve their own and others' images of them. They can teach students to accept and offer praise and criticism appropriately with others. Students may also need training in wearing clothing appropriate to different social situations and answering and using telephones properly. The more students master such social skills, the more self-confidence they will develop.

Personal and social skills

For all people with and without disabilities, it can be challenging to get along with others. One of the commonest reasons that adults are fired from jobs and students have problems in school is inadequate social and personal skills. Students with various disabilities that affect learning often do not learn through observation and imitation as others do. Teachers need to instruct them explicitly in areas like self-awareness. They must teach them to identify their own physical and psychological needs, abilities, interests, and emotions by asking them questions; showing them how to point to pictures representing various feelings, actions, events; or teaching them descriptive vocabulary. Teachers need to guide students to learn to identify and demonstrate knowledge of their physical beings and their relationship to and interaction with space, objects, and other people. They need to help students properly utilize, care for, and maintain hearing aids, glasses, braces, crutches, wheelchairs, or walkers. Teachers can also help disabled students learn appropriate strategies for coping with life stressors.

For students with disabilities to interact well with their classmates and others, one key area is in social conversations as well as in class discussions. Students must learn both to listen to others, which includes not only refraining from interrupting them, but also listening attentively to what they say, and to respond appropriately to what others say. Students with intellectual disabilities may, for example, change the subject completely instead of saying something that continues the topic. Teachers can give explicit instruction. For example, they can ask the student to repeat or paraphrase what another student just said; then ask her/him what possible things s/he could say in return on the same topic; have her/him demonstrate; and give positive reinforcement. Another area is forming and maintaining close relationships and friendships with others. Teachers can counsel students by asking them who shares particular interests, activities, and/or personal characteristics with them; helping them identify and implement behaviors for establishing and keeping relationships and friendships; and monitoring their progress by inquiring periodically.

Some students with cognitive disabilities may not have a good sense of personal possessions and boundaries. Consequently, they may take others' belongings; not take turns with others; or go ahead of others in lines. One facet of socially responsible behavior is respecting others' property and rights. Teachers can point out other students' showing such respect; explicitly show intellectually disabled students how to do the same; and give ample positive reinforcement whenever they do. Students with behavior disorders like oppositional defiant disorder will defy/ignore authority and directions. Teachers can establish behavioral contracts with them whereby they gain rewards meaningful to them for complying with clearly defined terms of what to do and not do. Students with ADHD easily act on impulse and become distracted, interfering with following directions. Behavior modification techniques or cognitive-behavioral therapy, sometimes in conjunction with medication, can help. Students also must learn to recognize valuable personal characteristics (e.g., honesty, kindness, or bravery); their personal roles in society; and social etiquette and proper behavior in public.

Independence for students with disabilities

Many students with disabilities have had things done for them that they could not accomplish alone and may have become habituated to passively waiting for others to initiate activities. Educators can help them achieve more independence by first explicitly teaching a student needed skills, giving prompts for each step, and then systematically fading the prompts so the student gradually performs tasks/activities with less and less help, direction, and guidance. Depending on the disability and activity, some students ultimately achieve full independence, while others can do more than before with less assistance. Students also must learn to take responsibility for their behaviors. Teachers/specialists can help students navigate the community by teaching orientation, mobility, street directionality, how to use public transportation, or strategies for coping with getting lost or with timetable changes when traveling. They can also teach them to follow safety procedures. They can counsel them in choosing friends and provide behavioral procedures for choosing clothing and getting to school on time.

Problem-solving skills for students with disabilities

As much as some students with disabilities may want to be completely independent, some disabilities dictate that they will need help with some things at times. A crucial behavior included among problem-solving skills is having the judgment, willingness, and ability to ask for help when they really need it. Educators can help in one on one, small group, or whole class settings by initiating discussions wherein students identify situations they have experienced when they needed help; what they did; what they could have done instead; and discriminate situations where they could have succeeded independently from those where this was impossible. Some students can benefit by learning from the experiences their classmates share. Teachers/specialists can assess and teach student skills for identifying problems, give them practice in predicting the consequences of events/actions, develop various alternatives for responding to problems, and evaluate their relative effectiveness. They can also work with students individually and in groups on developing their own goals, plans, and solutions to problems.

SWPBS

School-wide positive behavioral support program (SWPBS) is not a practice, intervention, or curriculum per se. It is rather an operating framework for decision-making, toward the goal of assuring access for all students to the most effective possible teaching and behavioral interventions and practices. It guides a school's choice, integration, and application of evidence-based best practices to realize all students' best academic and behavioral outcomes. Six principles guiding SWPBS are: establishing a continuum of behavioral and academic supports and interventions based on science; utilizing real data for problem-solving and decision-making; organizing environments to prevent problem behaviors from occurring or developing; encouraging and teaching pro-social behaviors and skills; accountability and fidelity in implementing evidence-based behavioral practices; and universal screening and continuous monitoring of student performance and progress. Four interrelated elements of SWPBS are: data for making decisions; measurable outcomes, which data evaluate and support; practices backed by evidence they attain from the outcomes; and systems that support implementing the practices with effectiveness and efficiency.

Four integrated parts of SWPBS programs are data, practices, systems, and outcomes. The data educators collect about students' academic and social behaviors support the decisions they make about the academic and behavioral interventions and practices to use. The practices educators choose have science-based evidence of being effective for achieving the educational outcomes they desire. These practices support the desired student behaviors. The systems that educators establish support the most effective and efficient implementation of their chosen practices. These systems support implementation by supporting the behavior of the school personnel. The desired outcomes educators identify are observable and measurable, and the data they collect support these measurements. The students' outcomes in turn support the students' academic achievement and social competence. Well-implemented SWPBS makes learning environments less dangerous, exclusionary, aversive, and reactive, and more preventive, inclusive, engaging, and responsive. Disciplinary and classroom management issues like lateness, attendance, and antisocial behavior are addressed. Student behaviors needing more specialized interventions receive better support. And all students' academic motivation and performance are optimized.

School-wide positive behavioral support programs are typically divided into tiers along a continuum, based on how students respond behaviorally to intervention. In the first tier, all students in the school/system/district are given positive behavioral supports, such as giving positive rewards to reinforce exemplary and acceptable academic and social behaviors, which are implemented by all staff members in all school settings. This universal tier is known as primary prevention. The second tier of secondary prevention is for students whose behaviors do not respond to the behavioral supports given in the first tier, putting them at risk for disciplinary issues. These students are placed in a specialized group, where they receive more intensive behavioral measures. The third tier of tertiary prevention is for students identified as being at high risk of antisocial behaviors resulting in disciplinary problems and possible harm to themselves and/or others. These students receive individualized behavior management plans that are the most specialized and utilize the most intensive interventions.

Communication and emergency situations

An important part of communicating with other people is being able to recognize emergency situations and respond timely and appropriately. This can be difficult for students with intellectual disabilities, behavior disorders, and other conditions. Among those who do not recognize an emergency situation, some will always require supervision, while others can be taught certain basics, such as the smell of smoke; the sight of fire, flooding, or a person needing emergency medical attention; and what to do, like calling 911. Some students with disabilities can recognize emergency situations but may panic. Educators can use explicit, systematic instruction, including task analysis steps and behavioral shaping and chaining, to help them develop strongly entrenched procedures to follow. With enough practice, repetition, and reinforcement, many students with disabilities can implement these series of behaviors instead of panicking. Students with autism spectrum disorders often need explicit instruction in the meanings/purposes of social cues (like facial expressions, vocal intonations, gestures, body language, and verbal expressions) and how to respond appropriately.

Problem-solving procedure to apply to conflict resolution

The teacher introduces the topic to students by explaining that where a conflict exists, a problem exists, and that having a way to think about and try to solve a problem helps. The teacher writes three steps on the board and goes over each step with the students: (1) Define the problem; (2) Brainstorm solutions; and (3) Choose a solution and act upon it. The teacher explains that before solving a problem, people must agree to work out the problem; that for problem-solving to work, they must agree not to call names, yell, or otherwise escalate the conflict. For step (1), the teacher encourages the students to define the problem in a way that does not place blame upon others. For step (2), the teacher encourages the students to think of as many possible solutions as they can. For step (3), the teacher advises the students that they should pick a "win-win" solution wherein all parties benefit and nobody loses.

To help younger and disabled students learn how to resolve conflicts, the teacher can first teach them a three-step problem-solving approach consisting of defining the problem, brainstorming solutions, and choosing and implementing a solution. The teacher then gives students a script for a "fight"/conflict and puppets if appropriate for the students, and then has some students volunteer to act out the conflict script. Then they review the problem-solving approach. Once students agree on one or more solutions, have the volunteer players act out their choice(s). Students who are able may then work in small groups to create and perform their own conflict resolution sketches for the class. The teacher then leads a class discussion, asking the students: (1) Which things in the sketches caused the conflict to escalate; (2) Which things people can say to each other to show they want to stop fighting and solve the problem; and (3) Whether any of the students have experienced similar conflicts in their own lives and how they resolved those conflicts.

ADLs and task analysis

Many of us take activities of daily living for granted. Because we have long ago learned to do them automatically, we do not realize how complex they actually are by involving many different steps. This complexity, however, can baffle special-needs students who have not achieved automaticity. Task analysis provides a solution by separating tasks into smaller,

- 60 -

more manageable steps. Educators must also provide support, like going over each step with the student to ensure their understanding; helping with steps the student cannot do independently; answering student questions; and monitoring that they complete all steps correctly and in the right sequence. Daily life skills tasks can easily be connected with general education curriculum. For example, reading care instruction tags on clothing and directions on soap packages when doing laundry and discussing it with others connect with English. Measuring laundry soap, reading washing machine and dryer dials and numbers, sorting and counting clothes, and estimating washing and drying times connect with mathematics. This also applies to cooking, meal preparation, etc.

To function independently in the home or community, special-needs students must learn such ADLs as selecting clothes suitable for the day's weather and activities; doing grocery shopping for the week; performing personal hygiene like toileting, bathing, brushing teeth, etc.; organizing and doing household chores; managing money and paying bills; taking out garbage and retrieving trash/recycling bins; cooking a simple meal; doing laundry; and others. Task analysis breaking a task down into individual steps is effective for special-needs students who otherwise have difficulty remembering all a task's parts and sequence. For example, doing laundry can be broken down into 10–12 steps. Before giving all steps to the student and supervising following them, the educator must follow these steps: Write down the steps, in chronological sequence. Assess what parts of steps the student can already do independently. Assess what steps/partial steps the student can do partly or with some adult assistance. Teach the student the steps that s/he cannot already do. Evaluate whether the instruction was effective for the student's learning.

Steps in task analysis for laundry
(1.) Take the laundry hamper to the laundry room. (2.) Empty the hamper onto the table/floor. (3.) Sort laundry into colors and whites. (4.) Open the washing machine. (5.) Put one sorted pile (or as much of it as will fit easily) into the washer. (6.) Add laundry soap. (7.) Turn on the washer. (8.) Wait until the machine is done. (9.) Open the washer. (10.) Take the laundry out and look to make sure everything is clean. (11.) If not, remove soiled pieces and put them back into the washer for another cycle. (12.) Put laundry in the dryer.* (13.) Choose the right setting for the fabric type. (14.) If needed, set the length of drying time. (15.) Turn the dryer on. *[Alternative: Hang laundry on the clothesline to dry.] (16.) When laundry is dry, remove each piece from the dryer/clothesline. (17.) Fold each piece and put it into the hamper. (18.) Put away the clean laundry in the right closets, drawers, etc.

Picture cards
Many special-needs students encounter difficulty processing information communicated verbally; initiating activities independently; maintaining attentional focus; and completing each step in a multiple-step task. When instructing special-needs students in ADLs, educators find a valuable resource in picture cards because these convey information visually instead of only verbally; they are naturally amenable to task analysis by using one picture card for each step in a task and arranging cards in the correct sequence; and they can be integrated into visual/graphic schedules, functional communication systems, and/or story strips. "Reminder strips" are short strips of picture cards that help students follow sequential steps when they cannot remember these without visual cues. For example, for hand-washing, a reminder strip placed above a sink can include individual pictures (with word captions) of turning on water, soap, lathering hands, turning off water, and drying hands on a towel, respectively. Many online resources offer printable cards, some designed

for students to color themselves, which increases their engagement, enjoyment, and ownership in the learning process.

Adaptive behavior skills

To increase progress toward independent living, two of many important areas are time management and hygiene. While parents commonly wake their children, when they get older teaching them to use an alarm clock/clock-radio frees them from depending on parents. For students with ASDs, parents may need some trial-and-error experimentation with different loudness, sounds (e.g., beeps or buzzes or music, and music types) as many are hypersensitive to sensory stimuli. For those capable, advanced skills include setting the alarm independently and deciding when to set an alarm for by estimating the time they need. Parents/educators can also teach students to use a watch/clock to manage home/school task completion. Students having difficulty with numbers can benefit from graphic visual timers. Students also need to develop hygiene routines for bathing, using deodorant, grooming, and dressing. Many ASD students naturally have rigid behavior, find routines comforting, and are amenable to daily bathing/showering (which is easier long-term than every 2–3 days) and specific instructions, like washing each area four times.

Preparation for independent living

To prepare children with disabilities for more independent living as they grow up, parents and educators can start teaching young children responsibility for their belongings. For example, when young children bring their toys with them in the car or to others' homes, they can be taught a routine to find the toy before leaving, take it to the car, and bring it inside when arriving at home. As they get older, this routine can be transferred to backpacks, school supplies, digital devices, and phones. Adults can also teach young children to employ visual cues for remembering duties. For example, they can keep medications in specific locations as reminders to take them at the specified times. They can use Post-it notes on their backpacks reminding them to pack lunch and/or bring permission slips and completed assignments to school. Adults can begin teaching food preparation and how to make noncooked snacks and sandwiches to young children. As they grow, adults can teach them to follow recipes, safely utilize kitchen tools, and cook.

Adults can help many students with cognitive, behavioral, emotional/social, and mental health disabilities prepare for daily life. For example, for telephone skills, they can first teach young children to answer the telephone, and then take and deliver messages. As they grow, adults can help them progress with skills like calling 411 for phone numbers; calling stores in advance to ask if they have certain products in stock; calling restaurants to order takeout or delivered food; or calling technical support for help with computer issues. Adults can teach young children about walking to nearby neighborhood places; teach middle children about riding bicycles to destinations and taking public transportation when ready; and help adolescents and young adults learn to drive when appropriate. They can teach children as they grow to carry house keys, cell phones with important numbers, and money when leaving home; and personal safety, like judgment about hand-shaking versus hugging/kissing; protecting their personal information online and money in public; and what to do if followed/approached by strangers.

Career awareness

When working with students with disabilities at the elementary school level, career development includes making students aware of workers in the community, and also helping them comprehend individual uniqueness, work's role in life, and fundamental knowledge about various jobs. Teachers can develop programs engaging students in activities involving adult workplaces and familiarize students with the kinds of social interactions they will experience after leaving school. Educators can also teach young students skills related to employment in the classroom, and then reinforce those skills in situations that expose them to workplace experience. Teachers can plan 1 to 3 hour field trips to visit different workplaces in their community. To prepare students, teachers can make them familiar with basic career information. After field trips, teachers can ask students questions like: What are the working environment and conditions? What abilities and skills do the jobs require? Do jobs observed primarily involve things, people, ideas, or information? Where/how can you learn skills for this occupation? Are you interested in this occupation? Why/why not?

To help prepare students with disabilities for futures in the workplace, educators can provide work experience in/around school. They can instruct them in doing laundry for the art room, gymnasium/pool, or lower grades' classrooms. Students can learn to sweep, vacuum, mop, wipe chairs and tables, and refill condiment containers in the cafeteria. Teachers can instruct students, sometimes with assistance from the custodial staff, in janitorial tasks like taking out garbage, dusting, cleaning, floor-waxing/buffing, painting, or refilling soap and paper towel dispensers. They can also enlist groundskeeper staff to help teach students seasonal outdoor tasks like weeding, mulching, mowing grass, and raking leaves. With the cooperation of office staff, teachers can instruct students in clerical tasks like preparing mail, making copies, filing, and data entry. Students can learn to help maintain school buses by vacuuming and washing. They can learn to restock vending machines; collect and count the money and deliver it; recycle materials; or construct and paint scenery and run lights for school plays/assemblies.

School-to-work training

President Clinton signed the School to Work Opportunities Act of 1994 (Public Law 103-239) into law. This law is a joint initiative by the U.S. Department of Education and Department of Labor. In transitions from school to work (STW), students with disabilities may need help with environmental accommodations; job accommodations; assistive technology devices; and additional supports for full participation in STW programs based in schools and/or communities. Key issues affecting success or failure in the workplace are related to social skills, for both nondisabled and disabled workers. In fact, 75 percent of job loss within the nondisabled population is attributed to poor social interactions. Disabled students also need good awareness of their own strengths and weaknesses to succeed at work, and skills for compensating for their deficits and making the most of their talents. Survey research with employers hiring disabled workers indicates that they want employees who are dependable, on time, can follow basic directions, and get along with their coworkers.

Some common STW curriculum subjects include employment-related functional academics; independent living skills; and interpersonal skills, since social skills are critical for nondisabled and disabled workers alike to get and keep jobs. Many opportunities connect school with work so students gain employment experience. Students can get unpaid/paid work experience through internships, structured for practically applying academic knowledge in jobs; job shadowing in one-day workplace visits and observing an employee in a specific job; or adult mentors, who serve as role models by communicating information about workplace norms, giving consistent, caring guidance and support, reviewing progress regularly, and establishing high expectations. Co-op programs combine technical and career classwork with part-time work during school years, with expectations for employers to provide and students to learn defined in training agreements. Community members visit schools on Career Days to share their experiences with interested students. Teachers can learn of academic job preparation through unpaid/paid workplace programs. Additional opportunities include apprenticeships, on-the-job training, field trips, class speakers, school-sponsored enterprises, and health care "clinicals."

Transition planning and Indicator 13

Transition planning helps students with disabilities and their families consider students' lives after high school; identify long-term goals; tailor high school learning for acquiring skills and contacts they will need to meet those goals; and with allocation to local school districts of funding and services supporting transition processes. Students and adults invest in students' future well-being by planning for postsecondary life. The IDEA's Indicator 13 is a provision that students with disabilities age 16 and above must have IEPs including postsecondary transition plans. The U.S. Department of Education's Office of Special Education Programs (OSEP) requires states to develop six-year State Performance Plans, based on about 20 indicators, and submit indicator data in Annual Performance Reports for Indicator 13 by February 2011. The National Secondary Transition Technical Assistance Center (NSTTAC) has developed the I-13 Checklist to aid state data collection. States may use their existing monitoring systems; however, this checklist can be used instead, or to evaluate those systems, or as a supplement, and is approved by the OSEP.

Postsecondary transition planning

The IDEA requires all students with disabilities to have postsecondary transition plans included in their IEPs when they are age 16 and older. When setting goals for students with disabilities to make transitions from school to work, job training and/or higher education, and community living, a few general criteria include that the goals should reflect expectations that are both high and realistic for the student. These goals should also reflect an approach for some kind of forward progress rather than a dead-end situation. When establishing postsecondary goals, the goals and objectives may be of mixed character, reflecting the ability, endurance, and stamina levels of the individual student. The transition plan can and should include external supports as needed. Transition plans can begin with more general goals and incorporate more specific details as the student comes closer to graduation. These goals may change from one school year to the next. Changes can range from minor alterations to major differences, depending on the individual student and situation.

When planning postsecondary transitions for significantly disabled students, adults should consider whether the student is able to express his/her interests. If not, educators should obtain information from parents/caregivers for planning transitions. They should consider the student's special health care needs. They must account for any challenges or needs that keep the student from working outside of home. Transition planners must determine who can provide training and/or education to help the student's transitions. They must determine what the student can already do without others' assistance. And they must also consider what else the student could do if s/he had help from a habilitation training specialist, a job coach, a caregiver, or other service provider(s). Additional ideas for transition planning include connecting students and their families with other students who have similar disabilities and their families; identifying peer mentors for students; supplying the resources the student needs; and inviting others who can make valuable contributions to join the transition planning team.

Vocational assessment and planning: Employment preparation for disabled students contains the same essential components as for nondisabled students: assessing and establishing skills; exposure to career possibilities; and awareness of aptitudes and interests. However, greater and more individualized supports for these components are involved with disabled students. Successful school-to-work transition programs require transdisciplinary, comprehensive vocational assessment to identify student skills and needs by teachers, psychologists, counselors, and representatives from vocational rehabilitation and social services agencies and community mental health/intellectual disabilities departments as well as the students, parents, employers, and business organizations. Assessment should cover academic, daily living, personal, social, occupational, and vocational skills (including performance tests and situational assessments); career maturity; vocational interests; and vocational aptitudes. A number of standardized instruments are available for assessing the latter two. Three major goals for students to learn in school activities for vocational preparation are: understanding themselves, their abilities, interests, and values; understanding the world of work; and learning good decision-making skills. These enable informed, realistic work-related decisions, and are also the main elements of career maturity.

Foundations and Professional Practice

History of disabilities and special education

Special education is a relatively new development in human history. Historically, people with disabilities received little or no education and were frequently placed into asylums or hospitals. The ancient Greek and Roman civilizations viewed disability as an evil omen, punishment from the gods. They viewed people as unable to change. Plato and Aristotle recommended euthanizing disabled infants. Cicero cited need for military superiority as reason to rid society of "defectives." The city/state took charge of soldiers disabled by combat. Due to ancient Greek and Roman philosophies, children born with disabilities were often drowned, "dashed against the rocks" as Homer described, thrown off cliffs, left to die on hilltops, chained up, or locked away. And fathers had the right to end a disabled child's life. In historical Christianity, while various physical ailments were treated as ritual impurities in the Old Testament, the New Testament shows Jesus healing the disabled, emphasizing their need for help and the goodness of helping them.

Middle Ages, the Renaissance, and the Enlightenment

In Medieval times (c. 500–1500 CE), society had a rigid caste system with royalty at the top, and no education for the masses. Some people with disabilities were exterminated; others were exploited as clowns, "fools," or servants. Generally, the disabled experienced ridicule for their differences. During the Renaissance (c. 1300–1700), when interest in knowledge was reborn, the Catholic Church made the disabled wards of the state, caring for them in isolation. They received more humane treatment, but initially no education. By the Enlightenment (c. 1650–1800), philosophers like John Locke believed all knowledge was acquired through the senses and all human beings were equal. Enlightenment philosophers believed humanity did not exist without education, increasing potential opportunities. During the Renaissance, in 1578, Spanish explorer Pedro Ponce de León first documented the education of royal deaf children. In 1760 during the Enlightenment, the French Abbé de L'Épée established the first institute for the deaf. In 1829 (the Regency era), Louis Braille invented his tactile reading/writing system for the blind.

Jean-Marc Gaspard Itard

Itard was a French doctor and educator, among the first to propose and prove special teaching methods could help educate children with disabilities. From 1801–1805, Itard used systematic instructional techniques to teach communication and daily living skills to a boy named Victor, discovered in the woods, seemingly without human rearing. Itard's work was made more famous by director/actor François Truffaut in his 1970 film *L'Enfant Sauvage* (*The Wild Child*). Itard's goals were to socialize Victor, improve his awareness of environmental stimuli, expose him to ideas, teach him to communicate, and advance his thinking from concrete/simple to abstract/complex. Some successes included increased regularity and control in Victor's eating, sleeping, and personal hygiene; improved senses of taste and touch; and increased range of interests. Victor learned to sequence objects and utter a few single-syllable words. However, he never developed connected speech or emotional attachments, and longed for his previous life. Some speculate Victor had intellectual disability or autism, which would also explain why he was likely abandoned at an early age.

Édouard Séguin

French doctor Séguin had studied with Jean-Marc Itard, who insisted that children with disabilities could learn via special instruction. In 1848 Séguin came to America, where he developed influential principles for educating intellectually disabled and other special-needs children. In his programs, he emphasized presenting combined physical and intellectual tasks to help disabled children develop self-reliance and independence. He developed the physiological method, consisting of sensory training (particularly tactile) utilizing concrete materials, and also motor training, featuring movement from the simple to the complex, age-appropriate and functional activities, and activities involving both work and play. The major elements that made up the foundation of Séguin's educational philosophy and programs for instructing children with disabilities were: frequently changing activities; task analysis; discrimination between the senses and the intellect; sensory stimulation; physical education; and education with employment as an outcome. One can see from these elements the importance of Séguin's contributions, as these are all still prominent aspects of special education today over 150 years later.

Maria Montessori

Maria Montessori (1870–1952), an Italian doctor and educator, developed an entire philosophy of education with procedures based on its principles. Today there are many Montessori schools worldwide. While the Montessori method is intended for the general education of all children, it has many benefits for children with disabilities and inclusive education. It is based on the way children naturally learn through exploring and experience. Montessori aimed to enable children's optimal exploration and independent learning. To this end, she proposed the concept of the "prepared environment," a learning environment designed to facilitate this learning process. This environment features an uninterrupted continuum of learning experiences. Montessori schools divide classrooms into multiple-age groups: parent and infant for ages 0–3; preschool, ages 3–6; lower elementary, ages 6–9 and upper elementary, ages 9–12; and middle school, ages 12–14. However, this series of classrooms comprise a "flow" experience, wherein the child continuously constructs and builds upon his/her learning throughout the program. Classroom materials each isolate various single qualities/concepts like color, shape, or size.

20th century

In the 1900s, the emphasis regarding disabilities was more biological than psychological or social. Hence many early pioneers of special education were both physicians and educators. Practitioners followed the medical model, and children with disabilities received institutional care. Between the 1900s and 1950s, laws made education compulsory, and educators created schools and classes for children who were blind, deaf, and mentally disabled. Following World War II, the special education system was established, with an organization parallel to the general education system. In the first of four main periods of special-needs education, children with blindness and deafness were most likely to receive instruction, while many children with other disabilities were still excluded from schools. In the second period, children with disabilities were segregated into homogeneous groups and received medical care and rehabilitation. The third period focused on normalizing and integrating the disabled into the community. In the fourth period, laws have mandated educational equality and inclusion rather than segregation in educational services for all children.

- 67 -

Characteristics of special education

Characteristics of "classic" special education include special settings; for example, segregated schools, classes, or resource rooms. Children are considered special, as evidenced by the way they are categorized, which determines their eligibility for special education and related services. "Classic" special education includes special teachers as well; whether they are trained and/or have experience or not, they are designated as special education teachers. Special education also includes therapists and other specialists trained to assess and remediate various conditions that qualify children for special education and related services. Special education traditionally involves a special teacher-student ratio: classes typically contain fewer students than general education classes, and more teachers per student. Another characteristic of special education is special teaching methods and tools; for example, Braille for the blind, sign language for the deaf, or communication boards/books/systems/software for the nonverbal. Special education also includes special goals, such as integration into the social life of the community, and special programs for teaching needed skills not normally needed by other students.

Advantages and disadvantages of segregated settings

In some cases, special schools and classes are still used today; however, in America and many other countries, laws mandate inclusive education for students with disabilities. Before this legislation, segregation was more the norm than the exception, yielding both advantages and disadvantages. Some advantages include: giving students with disabilities more chances of success; fostering cooperation instead of competition; being able to learn physical and social skills in accepting, understanding settings; staff with specialized training, specialized equipment, and specialized services; more opportunities to improve skills needed for greater participation in more inclusive settings; easier student access to individual attention; and more opportunities to meet other students with the same disability. Disadvantages include: developing "disabled" values, attitudes, and behaviors; lowered expectations in students, parents, and educators; resistance to transferring learned skills to regular settings; depriving disabled and nondisabled children of the benefits of interacting; less preparation for future living; greater lifelong expenses; more interactions with adults than with children; and performance standards separate from "normal" standards.

Medical model vs. social model

Historically, early models of special education were based on the medical model of illness. As special education developed, the medical model came to be gradually replaced by the social model. Some key differences in these models are: The medical model viewed the child as defective, whereas the social model values the child as a unique individual. The medical model focused on diagnosing and labeling children by their disabilities; the social model strives to identify children's strengths and needs. The medical model focused on impairment; the social model focuses on identifying obstacles and developing solutions. The medical model dictated segregation and alternative services for the disabled; the social model dictates making necessary resources available to the disabled within inclusive settings. The medical model resulted in being excluded permanently from normal schools and society, or inclusion only if the individual eventually seemed sufficiently "normal" in appearance and behavior; the social model welcomes diversity. The medical model effected no social change; the social model causes society to evolve.

Overrepresentation of certain groups in special education

For the past 30 plus years, court cases and other legal actions have been filed against the special education system over excessive placement of culturally and linguistically diverse students in disability programs. ESL, low-income, African-American, Latino, and Native American students are commonly overrepresented, particularly in programs for LDs, mild intellectual disabilities, and emotional/behavioral disorders. The National Center for Culturally Responsive Educational Systems (NCCREST) advises parents to consult school administrators and/or parent advocates to investigate whether their school has this problem, because researchers disagree about formulae for assessing overrepresentation. However, they also offer one formula for calculating overrepresentation probability: using low-income students as an example, divide their number placed in (for example) LD classes by their total number in the school = percent placed in LD; calculate the same percentage of average income students in LD classes the same way; and divide the low-income percentage by the average income percentage. A result of + 1.0 indicates equal probabilities of special education placement; > 1.0 indicates greater placement probability for lower income students.

Inclusion

Internationally, in 1948, the Universal Declaration of Human Rights addressed rights to inclusive education, as did the UN Convention on the Rights of the Child in 1989. In 1990, the World Declaration for Education for All addressed inclusion. In 1993, the Standard Rules on the Equalization of Opportunities for Persons with Disability established rights of disabled people to equal opportunities in education and employment. In 1994, UNESCO (the United Nations Educational, Scientific, and Cultural Organization) issued the Salamanca Statement and Framework for Action on every child's basic rights to education, stating that educational systems and programs should address children's diversities; special-needs students require adaptations enabling regular school access; and inclusive regular schools most effectively fight and prevent discrimination and make society inclusive. Significant U.S. laws include Section 504 of the 1973 Rehabilitation Act; the Education for all Handicapped Children Act (EHA) (1975/1986); the Americans with Disabilities Act (ADA, 1990); the Individuals with Disabilities Education Act (IDEA, 1997/2004); and the No Child Left Behind (NCLB, 2001) Act.

Recent and current trends related to technology, inclusion, and early intervention

Technological progress has afforded increased opportunities for both students and teachers in special education. Computer software programs enable students with speech and language and visual disabilities to convert text to speech; hearing-impaired students to convert speech to text; and ESL students to read translations in their native languages. Websites offer students more independent schoolwork at their own pace; multimodal presentations for LD students; and the ability for ADHD students to alternate among shorter units and topics. Students with auditory processing difficulties, and teachers needing more instructional materials, can access more graphic/visual stimuli online. The Internet also facilitates student/parent/teacher access to advocates, support groups, and organizations. Trends are increasingly toward inclusion, with more students mainstreamed than ever.

Special classes and schools exist when needs require/parents prefer, but the IDEA's LRE requirement moves more students into regular education classes/curricula/schools. Whereas learning disabilities were previously identified and services recommended in upper-elementary grades or later, today screening, assessment, identification, and intervention are advised by early childhood or even earlier.

Behavior management

The Council for Exceptional Children's Code of Ethics states this principle: "Special education professionals participate with other professionals and...parents in an interdisciplinary effort in the management of behavior." No one approach works with all students in all situations. While classroom management interventions may be ideally designed and implemented, not addressing individual children's needs and wants limits their effects. Hence one/several students in a class/setting may need behavior management strategies targeting specific behaviors. Cognitive interventions can affect emotional behaviors and psychomotor interventions can influence cognitive and affective development. Educators, parents, and others frequently ask about changing individual and group student behaviors; whether to punish or ignore behaviors; whether to discuss behaviors with students; and whether interventions are ethical, harmful, or effective. CEC suggests an educator activity like the following. Small groups list target behaviors and individual/group interventions, discussing whether these treat students with dignity, teach new skills, and support/need environmental analysis; whether student responses are clear to everybody, including students; whether educators respond sequentially to target behaviors (e.g., the second time a behavior occurs).

Classroom management and behavior management

According to researchers (e.g., Smith & Rivera, 1995), to establish/maintain classroom order, teachers should develop positive atmospheres and foundations of positive learning environments; use preventive techniques; develop collaboration with parents and other professionals around disciplinary issues; make sure interventions are appropriate to the problems they address; and regularly evaluate student progress. The goal of behavior management strategies is self-discipline, defined as gaining control over one's behavior in varied situations with various groups and individuals. Some ethical concerns include questions like these: Who decides who will manage behavior and whose behavior will be managed? How can others control behavior managers? Which interventions will be used, and who decides on accepted interventions? For what goals/purposes will interventions be implemented? Are/should children be free to make choices? Are student actions observable, measurable, repeated, and congruent with behavioral principles? In schools: Can externals—educators, peers, parents—change student behavior? Who decides which/whose behaviors to change? What interventions are used in classrooms? And who monitors them?

Under its ethical principle regarding behavior management, the Council for Exceptional Children (CEC) includes the following: (1) Professionals must use only behavioral procedures and disciplinary techniques they have been told to use, and that do not compromise individual student dignity or exceptional students' fundamental human rights (e.g., corporal punishment). (2) Professionals must specify clearly in the student's IEP any goals and objectives related to behavior management. (3) Professionals must comply with rules, statutes, and policies of state and local agencies regarding appropriately applying behavioral and disciplinary practices. (4) When they perceive a coworker's behavior as detrimental to special education students, professionals must take sufficient measures for preventing, discouraging, and intervening with those actions. (4) Professionals must avoid using aversive methods, unless repeated uses of other techniques were ineffective, and then only after consulting with parents and applicable agency officials.

Educators should always explore alternate behavioral interventions before considering any aversive methods. When considering/planning behavioral interventions, educators should first explore any possible injury or side effects these could cause. Before arranging contingencies to apply to student behaviors, educators should discern whether the student understands the contingency. Anyone implementing any behavioral intervention with a student must both have sufficient training in the procedures and feel comfortable applying the intervention. Interventions should be backed by empirical evidence of their effectiveness; be consistent with student programs and parental input; and have written informed parental consent. Behavioral intervention programs must be closely monitored and thoroughly documented. Procedures of legal due process and committee reviews should be followed. Behavioral interventions/programs should comply with the IDEA's Least Restrictive Environment requirement. Interventions should be commensurate with relative seriousness of the behavior; afford student opportunity to succeed; respect individual student worth and dignity; be fair; and address the principle of normalization (disabled students have rights to lives as close to normal as possible).

Legal requirements of school districts and legal rights of parents

Under current federal laws, all public school districts are required to invite parental participation in meetings regarding the evaluation, identification, and placement of their children in special education; notify parents in writing of any intentions to identify/assess/place their child in special education or change their identification/assessment/placement; notify parents in native languages/formats they understand; inform parents of resources available to help them understand written school notifications; and give parents copies of their legal rights and responsibilities and all procedural safeguards. Parents have the right to give written consent for referral, evaluation, re-evaluation, and placement in special education of their children; review all educational records regarding these; have interpreters supplied when they are not native English speakers; contribute input to all assessments, conversations, and decisions, initially and/or subsequently; request independent evaluations not paid by them if they disagree with district evaluation/diagnosis; participate in eligibility determination and placement; receive copies of evaluations, reports, and eligibility determination documents; and receive regular progress reports during their children's special education program placement.

Children's rights during behavior management process

According to the Council for Exceptional Children, children have rights in the areas of normalization, fairness, and respect. The principle of normalization means that a person with a disability has the right to develop a life that is as close as possible to that of normal persons. The principle of fairness includes not only basic fairness, but also the due process of law. Educators must determine whether a specific intervention they choose for modifying a student's behavior is fair to the student as an individual. The principle of respect means the student has the right to be treated as a human being rather than a statistic or an animal. Educators must measure any intervention in light of this principle. For example, physical or psychological punishment, segregation or isolation, medication, shock, restraints, or other punishments usually violate this principle. Ethics encompassing these principles dictate that in behavior management procedures, the means do NOT justify the end unless the principles of normalization, fairness, and respect have been met.

Confidentiality

The National Association of Special Education Teachers (NASET)'s Code of Ethics contains six principles. Principle 5 states: "NASET Members collaborate with parents of children with special needs and community, building trust and respecting confidentiality." Under this principle, subsection 5-E states, "NASET Members respect the private nature of the special knowledge they have about children and their families and use that knowledge only in the students' best interests." (2006/2007, NASET) The Family Educational Rights and Privacy Act (FERPA, 1974, aka Buckley Amendment) is the primary legislation delimiting accessibility and disclosure of student records. Privacy regarding student participation in evaluation, analysis, and surveys is defined by the Grassley Amendment (1994) to the Goals 2000: Educate America Act of 1994. Records of student drug and alcohol treatment kept by any entity receiving federal funding have protection under the Drug Abuse Office and Treatment Act (1976). In addition to these laws, the Individuals with Disabilities Education Act (IDEA, 1997/2004) protects the confidentiality of records for students receiving special education and related services.

Culturally and linguistically diverse students

School's climate and philosophy
A school's principal should advocate strongly for the well-being and interests of culturally and linguistically diverse students receiving special education and related services. Parents and teachers should consider how the principal shows her/his commitment in this respect. A school's curriculum should reflect the viewpoints, contributions, and experiences of diverse linguistic and ethnic groups. Parents should consider whether a school's principal and staff blame diverse students or their families for different educational performance levels, and whether schools pressure diverse families to embrace school values, or work to incorporate cultural and language differences into their instructional programs. It is important to look for ways in which school administrators and staff demonstrate respect for language and cultural differences. Parents will want to consider whether the environment of a given school is orderly and safe for their children. Additionally, a school should demonstrate high expectations and provide sufficient achievable curricular challenges, both supported by evidence, for all of its students.

Approaches to prevent unnecessary referrals to special education
A school should recognize and incorporate cultural and linguistic differences in their practices related to assessment, curriculum planning and design, and instruction. Considering the demographics of American society today, all/most schools should have ESL programs. Classroom instruction and other school functions should include languages other than English. Schools should have support systems in addition to special education, such as tutoring programs, teacher assistance teams, and bilingual education programs. Schools should collaborate with their communities in established programs. They should also support their teachers via professional development offerings that respond to needs expressed by faculty members and continuing collaboration and consultation of teachers with other professionals. Educators should build upon students' existing knowledge and use

interactive discourse to promote both fundamental and higher order student skills for reading, math, and writing. Schools should systematically and continually evaluate student progress and the quality of their programs. Decision-making should include all relevant stakeholders. School educators should include cooperative learning methods and thematic instructional techniques in their teaching.

Assessment

The assessment stage is when professionals collect data used to determine or rule out disability; therefore, parents and cultural diversity experts should be included in the assessment team. Assessment plans should always include multiple instruments and settings to be comprehensive and reflect multiple perspectives and approaches. How student difficulties are addressed and what consequences result across various settings should also be considered. Suspected disabilities in ELLs should be assessed in a student's dominant language. Educators should gather data on student proficiency and educational achievement in both his/her first language and English. Assessment teams must obtain parental perceptions, beliefs, values, and expectations about children's learning/behavioral challenges. Schools should avoid interpreters and test translations. However, if these are unavoidable, they should document interpreter skills; ensure multiple formal and informal assessments and information sources; use peers from normative groups; and, if tests are invalidated, seek performance patterns rather than absolute scores. With behavioral referrals, educators should consider obtaining more information to corroborate interpretations of projective instruments, which can be subjective.

Eligibility determination and placement

Parents of culturally and linguistically diverse backgrounds should become involved in all stages of the special education process if their children are referred. In addition to being included on referral and assessment teams, parents as well as cultural diversity experts should be included in decision-making for eligibility determination and placement. This team should consider whether a student's difficulties are caused by a possible disability, cultural/social differences, or both. Immigration, switching schools, and school absences should be considered. Evidence of different sources of student difficulty should be provided. If a student is identified with a disability, parents should determine whether the school has specific plans for reviewing the student's circumstances in the future, determining whether the student might be reclassified. If a student is determined eligible for special education, parents should know whether team members work for placement in the least restrictive environment and seek proof/evidence of such efforts. They should find out if students with the same disability type and age are placed in similar programs and why..

Special education referral process

Because diverse students are frequently overrepresented in special education referrals, their parents should be included on referral teams, as well as persons with expertise regarding cultural diversity. Educators should review these factors before recommending comprehensive evaluations: the school and classroom climate; all attempts at pre-referral intervention and their results; any temporary problems in the classroom, home, and/or community; educator effort in building on students' cultural experiences and knowledge and their strengths; and observations by parents when possible, and by qualified others with knowledge of cultural differences, of the student's current classroom—particularly if the referral is for behavior management, as these problems can be influenced by teacher behavior management approaches. In addition, it is only appropriate to refer ESL/ELL students if: students have good communication skills in their native languages but are behind peers in English, and instructional adaptations have been implemented; students are academically proficient in English, receive effective reading instruction, and still demonstrate significant reading problems; and/or effective ESL or bilingual instruction do not improve academic English-language skills.

Collaboration between special educators and general educators

As all teachers have various strengths and needs, special educators should share these. General educators are likely less familiar with specialized resources for matching practices to student skill levels when these are far beneath grade level; special educators are likely less acquainted with the richness of grade-level projects and activities. Both types of teachers can pool their knowledge of proactive/preventive and disciplinary techniques, and two pairs of eyes can better prevent misbehavior and identify desirable behavior to reinforce. General educators have training in using and instructing students with many kinds of software; special educators contribute working familiarity with assistive technology. For routine planning, special and general educators can help each other develop simple student routines. While structure and content often easily combine in general education, special-needs students must learn how assignment directions are structured before addressing assignment contents. Teachers can use tracing/matching routines to plan independent student activities. Praise motivates teachers as well as students: collaborating special and general educators should regularly praise each other's successes verbally.

When collaborating, teachers must schedule *at least* one weekly planning session, even if it must be after school. Co-teachers will fail through unmet expectations and lack of communication without such planning. As in any relationship, co-teachers do not know everything about one another. They must share their ideas and experiences, not only to succeed in teaching their students, but to understand their own teaching and learning processes and to experience job satisfaction. Teacher collaboration processes will undergo changes, just as students discover new concepts over time through their teachers and their instructional methods. While these changes mean that co-teachers and students alike will encounter surprises and adjustments, they also mean that teachers will develop better ways of meeting student needs. Collaboration also affords teachers new perspectives. They can take advantage of these by making focused observations and asking reflective questions whenever not directly occupied in instructional delivery. Taking brief but specific notes helps co-teachers discuss observations later, troubleshoot/problem-solve, fine-tune instruction, and communicate student successes.

Regardless of which co-teacher is leading a lesson/activity at the time, both should be actively interacting with students, which includes physical movement: one's viewpoint is narrowed when sitting at one's desk/in a classroom corner, whereas moving about enables a global view. Co-teachers should determine shared organizational goals and periodically review these. During the school year, considering organization is often sacrificed under time pressures; however, small enhancements in organization can have major influences. Co-teachers can examine their total classroom environment for smooth flow of activities and how well students stay organized. Special educators can contribute techniques to establish regular external structures for students with deficits in executive functioning who do not generate such structure internally. They can help general education teachers with monitoring students and supporting their organizational needs through simple structures incorporating task analysis for following step-by-step routines, visual cues, and instruction in self-monitoring routines. Co-teachers should reflect on their entire process, analyze it,

- 74 -

and respond. They can experiment with co-teaching methods they could not use individually.

Curriculum and data collection

Many special educators, such as special education resource teachers, often teach students in multiple grades. To support their students' various educational needs, the special education teacher must know the general education curriculum. When this teacher works with multiple grade levels, s/he has to know multiple different curricula. This teacher must also collaborate with all students' general classroom teachers to ensure s/he supports what they teach. This entails both making time and being organized to speak with each teacher individually. Special education teachers must also provide data for each student, to document instruction that implements the student's IEP and document their reports of student success or difficulty in each area. They must monitor data collection, analyze data, and adjust instruction accordingly. They need the cooperation of general education teachers in collecting data when they are not in the general classrooms with students. While parents/others may volunteer to help collect data, special education confidentiality laws can prohibit volunteers without permission from the parents of every student in class.

Communicating and collaborating with community agencies

When special education students have already had interactions with some government departments like the juvenile justice system, the mental health system, or the department of social services, those agencies may initiate contact with schools/teachers. In other cases, educators may need to contact them. Community agencies dedicated to children with disabilities and all those working with/for them serve as liaisons/links to public and private schools and government departments, local officials, and legislators. Some community agencies offer services like direct representation; educators can invite them to IEP meetings and due process mediations and hearings on behalf of disabled students and their families to ensure effective advocacy, information, and support. Teachers can help get parents training on their rights and special education services from community agencies. Community agencies can provide professional educators and families with consultations on technical assistance for students with disabilities. If parents and school districts disagree, educators can enlist mediation services from some community agencies to prevent escalation into court cases.

Working with other professionals, teaching aides, assistants, and paraprofessionals

When educational research investigates high turnover rates among special educators, some researchers have thought the voluminous paperwork in special education was responsible, only to hear from some special education teachers that they attribute turnover more to being appreciated less than general education teachers. Special education teachers often must coordinate their schedules with art teachers, music teachers, physical education teachers, and 10–20 other teachers, and also show consideration to physical therapists, occupational therapists, and speech-language pathologists, as well as accounting for lunch and recess when making resource schedules. Even minor changes in general education teachers' schedules can alter the special education teacher's whole day or week. Most special education teachers are enormously grateful to their aides, assistants, and paraprofessionals; however, the reality is they must also devote significantly more time and effort to train them and create daily schedules for them. A teacher's aide differing in opinion from the teacher's, especially if the aide is older/more experienced than the teacher, presents an additional challenge to teamwork, for which the teacher is responsible.

Standards for credentials and employment of special education professionals

Some of the Council for Exceptional Children practice standards for special education professionals in credentials and employment include: represent oneself accurately, legally, and ethically regarding their expertise and knowledge to prospective employers; assure that those representing themselves and/or practicing as special education administrators, teachers, and related service providers have the qualifications of professional credentials; operate within their limits of professional skills and knowledge, and appropriately seek consultation and/or support from sources outside themselves as necessary; comply with contractual terms of employment; comply with policies and contracts of local education agencies for notifying them when terminating their positions; advocate for supportive and suitable educational conditions, and for staffing resources sufficient to keep absences of support staff or substitute teachers from causing special education services to be denied; and get professional help for personal problems affecting work performance.

In addition to nine others, the CEC (Council for Exceptional Children) identifies standards for special education professionals that include: documenting and reporting objectively any deficits in resources, and offering solutions for these to their supervisors/administrators; evaluating employment applicants and grievances objectively, without discrimination; utilizing established procedures to resolve professional workplace problems; expecting their responsibilities to be conveyed to coworkers, and assuring their understanding and respect of those responsibilities; requesting clear written statements of their employment conditions, duties, and responsibilities; participating actively in planning, management, and evaluation of special education programs and general education programs, and in associated policy development; expecting sufficient support and supervision for special education professionals, and for programs delivered by qualified professionals in special education; and expecting there to be clearly defined chains of accountability and responsibility regarding the supervision and administration of professionals in special education.

Professional development

Special education professionals cannot allow their training, knowledge, and expertise to remain at the same level throughout their working lives as when they received their degrees and certification and began working. They must continually update, improve, and expand their skills, both to remain current in this dynamic, changing profession and to grow as educators. Special education professionals acquire and apply knowledge about developmental levels and readiness for various instructional interventions. They learn about research evidence-based instructional strategies, and then apply these for teaching fundamental skills in literacy and numeracy to students with special needs. They know how to individualize their instruction for each student, and they continue to learn new strategies and techniques to improve this individualization process. They assess student progress on an ongoing basis and refine their assessment techniques to increase their accuracy and applications to adjustments and modifications in their instructional approaches. They make use of data and continually inform themselves of newer data from emergent research to apply to their problem-solving endeavors. They prepare students to become independent.

In the area of professional development, the Council for Exceptional Children (CEC) has standards that include: systematically keeping individualized plans for their own professional development, designing these to increase their own skills, knowledge, and cultural competence to sustain high competency levels; keeping current in their knowledge of laws, policies, and procedures related to their practices; systematically and objectively evaluating themselves, their coworkers, and their programs and services to enhance their professional performance continually; advocating for effective, schoolwide professional development and individual professional development plans being provided by their employing agencies; participating in supervised, systematic field experiences for special education professional candidates as a part of their educator preparation degree and certification programs; and functioning as mentors for other special educators in whichever times, places, and circumstances that their doing so is appropriate.

A number of organizations offer professional development courses. For example, the National Association of Special Education Teachers (NASET) has many classes. Professionals can learn more about modifications for alternative assessments; the annual and triennial review processes; assistive technologies for students with disabilities; ADHD, anxiety disorders, autism, pervasive developmental disorders, bipolar disorder, depression, Down syndrome, eating disorders, emotional disturbances, epilepsy, LDs, intellectual disabilities, orthopedic impairments, multiple disabilities, PTSD, Rett syndrome, schizophrenia, speech-language disorders, spina bifida, Tourette syndrome, traumatic brain injuries, blindness and visual impairments, deafness and hearing impairments, and deaf-blindness; auditory processing disorders; developmental and psychological disorders in special education; criteria for eligibility determination for special education services related to each disability; educational implications of some disorders; factors influencing curriculum for special-needs students; identification of high-risk students in classrooms; developing, writing, implementing, reviewing, and modifying IEPs; medications; services related to special education; team transitional planning; and helping students cope with disasters and violence.

Self-assessments

Many school districts and systems have created self-assessment rubrics or instruments for special educators. These instruments generally list specific standards for an array of required skills and knowledge, including operational definitions that describe what knowledge, skills, and behaviors the special educator should demonstrate. These descriptions are accompanied by incremental rating scales. The educator reads each competency and checks a box corresponding to whether s/he thinks s/he, for example, models it, adjusts upon reflecting, and is a resource for others (the highest score); or works independently to apply the competency across settings and self-initiates planning (the second highest); applies the competency with support and shows emerging self-initiation of planning (the middle score); understands and tries to apply the competency, and uses resources for improving his/her teaching (the second lowest); or is aware of the competency but has no experience in and/or does not demonstrate it (the lowest score). Another example states competence areas for self-rating as highly effective, effective, minimally effective, or ineffective.

Strategies to reflect on effectiveness of work

Research finds viewing video recordings of their teaching practices in combination with collaborative professional development courses and activities helps teachers enhance and change their practices. In one pilot study (Osipova, et al, 2011) teachers viewed many video recordings of themselves teaching throughout the school year. They self-reflected, noting what they did effectively, generating suggestions for future teaching, and rating their instruction. The researchers found this process altered teachers' initial self-reflections overestimating their practices to more critical self-examinations. It changed teachers' self-reflection comments, vague at first, to more specific descriptions. Teachers particularly realized they attended to certain students and not others. Because not all teachers apply what they learn in professional development to their classroom practices, researchers find guided/coached critical self-reflection instrumental for changing teacher beliefs about learning and teaching, which are frequently unspoken and even unconscious. Teachers are more likely to change their practices once they change their beliefs, and also when they view themselves as learners. Video self-reflection affords self-analyses with multiple foci, and also repeated self-analyses of teaching practices.

Practice Test

Practice Questions

1. Which of the following is the best sign that a child is developing the ability to perform abstract mental operations?
   a. Object permanence
   b. Egocentrism
   c. Pretend play
   d. Reversibility

2. In behaviorism, which of the following has been found most effective to increase a desired behavior?
   a. Positive reinforcement
   b. Negative reinforcement
   c. Positive punishment
   d. Response extinction

3. Cara wants all her cookies, but she also wants her best friend, who has no cookies, to be happy. These conflicting desires cause discomfort. She resolves this by sharing: she makes her friend happy and still has cookies for herself. This best illustrates which of these theories of motivation?
   a. Attribution Theory
   b. Expectancy Theory
   c. Cognitive Dissonance
   d. Extrinsic Motivation

4. A diagnosis of intellectual disabilities in a student requires which of the following evaluation results?
   a. Intellectual deficits indicated by IQ test scores
   b. Deficits in both intellectual and adaptive skills
   c. Adaptive behavior deficits with daily living skills
   d. Achievement deficits in academic performance

5. Which of the following characteristics are most typical of a student diagnosed with autism?
   a. Difficulty initiating and maintaining social interactions
   b. Difficulty focusing and maintaining attention to tasks
   c. Difficulty understanding abstract intellectual concepts
   d. Difficulty sitting still and staying quiet for long periods

6. Which of the following is true regarding individuals with developmental disabilities today?
   a. Their life expectancies have not increased the way those of nondisabled people have.
   b. The majority of funding for developmental disabilities is allocated for family support.
   c. Mandated school services have increased expectations of support for aging at home.
   d. Adults with developmental disabilities are not at higher risk for chronic health issues.

7. Which of the following is an example of disproportional representation of culturally and linguistically diverse (CLD) students in special education programs?
    a. CLD students' being overidentified as having developmental disabilities
    b. More CLD students' being categorized with emotional disturbance or intellectual disabilities
    c. CLD students in more restrictive programs than other special ed. students
    d. These are all examples of disproportional representation of CLD students.

8. Cathy has coexisting conditions of spina bifida and related health problems, intellectual disabilities, deafness, and autism. She engages in self-injurious behavior in response to physical distress. Which of the following is most likely true?
    a. The self-injurious behavior is an aberration that serves no purpose.
    b. The self-injurious behavior is an attempt to communicate a need.
    c. The self-injurious behavior is caused by her intellectual disabilities.
    d. The self-injurious behavior is caused by her autism diagnosis.

9. According to Bowen's Family Systems Theory, which is typical of the basic family relationship pattern when a child has a disability or impairment?
    a. Excessive parental anxiety engenders the disabled child's corresponding excessive anxiety.
    b. Parental focus on the disabled child increases the child's differentiation of self from family.
    c. The child with the disability experiences less reaction than siblings to parental expectations.
    d. Family tensions are less likely to be internalized or externalized by the child with a disability.

10. Which of the following is most accurate regarding environmental influences on the development and achievement of students with developmental disabilities?
    a. Environmental adaptations, modifications, and interventions are not advised for DD students.
    b. Teachers should not have high expectations of DD students, as this will only cause frustration.
    c. Access to academic rigor and realistic but high expectations enable DD students' higher achievement.
    d. Students with DDs should never be placed into academically rigorous educational programs.

11. Which of the following best describes Down syndrome?
    a. Gland malfunction
    b. Dominant-gene transmission
    c. Congenital deformity
    d. Chromosomal difference

12. What is Piaget's phrase for the strict and unwavering adherence to a rule?
    a. Ethical idealism
    b. Naturism
    c. Moral realism
    d. Constructivism

13. Approximately what percentage of the population is classified as intellectually disabled?
   a. Less than 1%
   b. 1 to 2%
   c. 2 to 3%
   d. 3 to 4%

14. For a teacher, what is the most common indicator that a student has a learning disability?
   a. Difference between measures of potential and achievement
   b. Difficulty concentrating
   c. Spelling mistakes
   d. Lack of physical coordination

15. Which of the following is NOT a possible symptom of rubella?
   a. Deafness
   b. Scoliosis
   c. Intellectual disabilities
   d. Cataracts

16. Judy has moderate intellectual disabilities, good expressive verbal skills, and extreme temper tantrums. During a tantrum at home one day, she slaps her roommate, who did nothing to provoke it. This reflects a need for remediation in which area?
   a. Affective behavior
   b. Self-esteem issues
   c. Self-concept issues
   d. Communication

17. IDEA's definition of intellectual disabilities includes "significantly subaverage general intellectual functioning" as well as which of the following?
   a. Concurrent deficiencies in adaptive behavior
   b. Adverse effects on educational performance
   c. Manifestation during the developmental period
   d. All of the above are part of the definition.

18. Which of the following is NOT primarily an assessment of adaptive skills?
   a. The Walker-McConnell
   b. The Vineland
   c. The WISC-IV
   d. The SSRS

19. The majority of people with intellectual disabilities have what level of intellectual disabilities?
   a. Mild
   b. Moderate
   c. Severe
   d. Profound

20. When writing learning objectives for a lesson plan, the S in SMART stands for Specific: an objective should specify what students will achieve and in what amount. Which of the following correctly identifies one of the other initials in the SMART acronym?
a. M stands for Memorable
b. A stands for Activities
c. R stands for Resources
d. T stands for Time-based

21. In a lesson plan, which of the following would NOT be included in the Instructional Procedures section?
a. Opening
b. Engagement
c. Assessment
d. Closure

22. Which of the following is correct regarding lesson plans and assessment of student learning?
a. The lesson plan should specify what kind(s) of summative assessment(s) will be used.
b. The lesson plan should specify what kind(s) of formative assessment(s) will be used.
c. The lesson plan should specify objectives and instruction but not include assessment.
d. The lesson plan should specify the formative and summative assessments to be used.

23. Of the following, which is the best example of a learning objective in a lesson plan?
a. John will demonstrate that he is able to read and comprehend at his grade level.
b. John will score at least 80% on all specified reading comprehension tests by June 1.
c. John will be able to read all grade-level materials, demonstrating 100% comprehension.
d. John will complete the assigned activity for reading and comprehending grade-level materials.

24. Which of the following is most applicable to providing access to the curriculum for a student who is hard of hearing?
a. Speech-to-text software
b. Text-to-speech software
c. Magnification of the text
d. Text with enlarged print

25. Of the following, which is true regarding access to the general curriculum (AGC) for disabled students?
a. General education classrooms' being more inclusive automatically gives disabled students more AGC.
b. The law requires AGC for special education students, but not students' active involvement in the GC.
c. The law requires AGC and active involvement in the GC for disabled students, but not their progress.
d. The law requires AGC for disabled students, their active involvement, and their progress in the GC.

26. Which of these is an advisable teacher strategy in organizing the learning environment to make it inclusive for students with disabilities as well as nondisabled students?
    a. Decorating the classroom with as many bright colors, pictures, and furniture as possible
    b. Storing books, manipulative objects, and other materials on high shelves to protect them
    c. Creating an area as a "meeting spot" within the classroom where all of the students can gather
    d. Placing students' desks far apart from one another to prevent students' distracting each other

27. Janice has a diagnosis of intellectual disabilities and is nonverbal. When she needs the teacher's help, she shrieks. Which of the following is the best strategy for managing this behavior?
    a. Training Janice to raise her hand or wave her arm to get the teacher's attention
    b. Consistently applying punishment every time Janice shrieks until she stops this
    c. Consistently ignoring the shrieking behavior until it is eventually extinguished
    d. Giving Janice constant teacher attention so she no longer has need to shriek

28. Jimmy's behaviors disrupt his classroom daily. What is the first step the teacher and other school staff should take?
    a. Refer Jimmy to receive special education services for a conduct or behavior disorder.
    b. Conduct a functional behavior analysis to determine the purpose(s) of the behaviors.
    c. Transfer Jimmy to a separate classroom reserved for students with behavior problems.
    d. Recommend to parents that Jimmy be placed in a special school for problem students.

29. Which of the following teacher ways of creating supportive learning environments for students is exemplified best by combining paired and small group activities with whole-class activities?
    a. Building students' senses of self-esteem and self-efficacy
    b. Building a strong classroom community for the students
    c. Communicating positive messages via nonverbal behaviors
    d. Motivating students by engaging their active participation

30. The continuum of alternative placements required by IDEA 2004 to meet special education needs must include those in IDEA's definition of special education. One of these alternative placements is instruction in special classes. Which of the following is NOT another alternative placement included?
    a. Instruction in special schools
    b. Instruction in regular schools
    c. Instruction given in hospitals
    d. All of the above are alternatives

31. Which of the following is NOT defined as a supplementary service by IDEA?
    a. Resource room instruction
    b. Itinerant staff instruction
    c. Mainstreamed instruction
    d. None of the above is defined as a supplementary service

32. Which of these is accurate regarding psychometric vs. developmental approaches to learning?

    a. Psychometric approaches see individual performance variations as showing amounts of ability.

    b. Psychometric approaches view individual performance variations as showing rates of growth.

    c. Developmental approaches seek to match students according to their equal levels of abilities.

    d. Developmental approaches seek to match curricula with the levels of their students' abilities.

33. Which of the following best represents a developmental philosophy of education?

    a. Learning is regulated by a group of principles, such as reinforcement.

    b. Learning is made up of acquiring sets of skills, independent of content.

    c. Learning involves problem-solving strategies, determined by content.

    d. Learning involves spontaneous, automatic transfer among subjects.

34. Of the following instructional strategies used, which is most likely to support LD students in taking risks during reading lessons in a large group/class setting?

    a. Assigning students to pairs to discuss teacher questions about the lesson

    b. Asking students to give summaries reviewing the main points of a lesson

    c. Having students complete reminder worksheets at the end of the lesson

    d. Inviting students to ask "who," what," or "where" questions on a lesson

35. Which of the following is a valid argument in favor of providing 1:1 instruction for students who are failing to learn to read?

    a. Special educators often have caseloads of many students requiring services for hours each day.

    b. Instruction using 1:1 methods is found by research studies to be very effective for LD students.

    c. Special educators are required more and more to teach collaboratively with classroom teachers.

    d. Increasing mandates of record-keeping enhance service documentation, not implementation.

36. Which is true about developmentally disabled students' transfer and maintenance of learning?

    a. Instructional tasks and settings should resemble application tasks and settings.

    b. Students should first acquire a skill, then gain fluency in it, and then transfer it.

    c. Applying a skill should be done uniformly, without discriminating among cases.

    d. Students should not practice fundamental skills until these become automatic.

37. Which of these is typical of most models of research-based interventions for individual students?

    a. Emotional, social, and behavioral supports target individual students rather than whole schools.

    b. Students above and below grade level, ELLs, and DD learners receive differentiated instruction.

    c. Research-based intervention removes targeted students from the general education classroom.

    d. Research-based intervention monitors student progress via infrequent, thorough assessments.

38. Stan is a young man with mild intellectual disabilities. He can perform all self-care routines, knows the meanings of common public and street signs, and can count money and make change. He has otherwise lived a sheltered life, never working for pay or visiting a workplace. Which of the following supplemental curricula is likely most important for him to become as independent as possible?

    a. Daily living activities

    b. Functional academics

    c. Employment training

    d. All are equally needed.

39. Which of the following pieces of adaptive equipment could help ALL of the following students: one with hearing impairment, one with communication deficits, one with cognitive deficits, and one with fine-motor skills deficits?

    a. A computer with a touch screen

    b. A classroom amplification system

    c. A large-print book/books on tape

    d. A word processor with voice output

40. Sue has moderate intellectual disability and can perform manual labor tasks with supervision. She currently attends a day training center. A local program offers paying work she could do with prompting. Which of the following is the best strategy to support a transition goal for Sue to progress from school to work?

    a. Continue to attend school, but shift instruction to focus more on job tasks and counseling

    b. Discontinue attending school and start employment with the local program independently

    c. Continue school half the time and work at the job half the time, supported by a job coach

    d. Discontinue attending school and begin employment with the program under supervision

41. Which of the following is an example of a preventive strategy for an at-risk student?

    a. Short-term targeted intervention

    b. School-wide behavioral supports

    c. Intensive individualized intervention

    d. Referral for Special Education evaluation

42. Which of the following does Vygotsky's term "scaffolding" refer to?
    a. A structural framework that a teacher creates for a lesson
    b. Support that is always present for a child with special needs
    c. An organizational structure that guides social interactions
    d. Support that is gradually withdrawn as independence grows

43. A teacher has a small class of students with intellectual disabilities who demonstrate very good behavior during any individual activity, but display a variety of problem behaviors whenever she switches to the next activity. Which of the following changes is MOST likely to address this issue?
    a. Making all of the activities much shorter in duration
    b. Scheduling a rest break after each individual activity
    c. Creating a transition from every activity to the next
    d. Asking for each student to have a behavior program

44. Introducing each of the stages of career development for students with disabilities should be determined *most* by which of the following?
    a. The student's developmental level
    b. The student's grade level in school
    c. The student's level of experience
    d. The student's chronological age

45. For a student with a mental age of approximately five years, which of the following would be the MOST effective strategy in a program designed to help him become independent in his self-care routines?
    a. Setting up a token economy
    b. Having him make checklists
    c. Playing him a self-care DVD
    d. Giving ongoing verbal prompts

46. Which of the following is the best example of an evidence-based assessment of a student's basic
writing skills?
    a. Test of Written Language (TOWL)
    b. Informal observation by teacher
    c. A classroom writing inventory
    d. A rubric-based assessment

47. Which statement is most accurate regarding the Cross-Battery Assessment (XBA) approach?
    a. It is an approach to testing for reading and writing disorders that is not evidence-based.
    b. It is an approach to testing students across different domains of academic achievement.
    c. It is an approach to testing students across different domains of intellectual competence.
    d. It is an approach to testing that can enhance comprehensiveness, selectivity, and depth.

48. Of the following instruments, which does not require the student to give any oral responses?
    a. The Wechsler Preschool and Primary Scales of Intelligence (WPPSI)
    b. The Peabody Picture Vocabulary Test (PPVT)
    c. The Stanford-Binet Intelligence Scales (SB)
    d. The Wechsler Intelligence Scales for Children (WISC)

49. Which of the following intelligence tests depends most on a student's verbal ability?
    a. UNIT
    b. TONI
    c. WIAT
    d. Raven

50. Of the following IQ measures, which would be most appropriate for an autistic student with verbal deficits?
    a. Leiter
    b. WISC
    c. Woodcock-Johnson
    d. RIAS

51. You want to interpret the results of a student's responses on the WISC-IV. Which of the following is correct regarding the FSIQ?
    a. The FSIQ is the average of all of the subtest scores.
    b. The FSIQ is the sum of the test's four index scores.
    c. The FSIQ is a separate score unrelated to subtests.
    d. The FSIQ is a measure not used by Wechsler tests.

52. The psychologist's interpretation of a student's test results gives very different levels of cognitive functioning vs. adaptive functioning. Which choice represents what these mean?
    a. Cognitive functioning is the student's ability; adaptive functioning is the student's performance.
    b. Cognitive functioning is the student's abstract thinking; adaptive functioning is concrete thought.
    c. Cognitive functioning is the student's intelligence; adaptive functioning is independent living skills.
    d. Cognitive functioning is the student's potential; adaptive functioning is the student's achievement.

53. A student was referred for a complete evaluation to determine eligibility for Special Education Services. Tests yield levels of cognitive and adaptive functioning. Which of the following is correct about how these results may be used?
    a. They may be used in describing the student's Present Level of Functioning on the student's IEP.
    b. They may be used as baselines to compare later scores in assessing program effectiveness.
    c. They may be used to determine the student's levels for placement in Special Education services.
    d. They may be used for any or all these purposes in making educational decisions for the student.

54. Jack's tests reveal: He has above-average intelligence and ability in both verbal and quantitative areas, despite difficulty getting him to sit still and attend during testing. He is not "acting out" to get attention, escape class, or vent emotions. He exhibits a short attention span, distractibility, difficulty focusing, and impulsive behavior. Which of the following is the best application of these findings?

    a. Refer Jack for a full psychiatric evaluation for a possible diagnosis of a major mental illness.

    b. Jack needs a behavior specialist/psychologist to write him a behavior management program.

    c. Jack needs not psychiatric testing or behavior management, but stronger disciplinary action.

    d. Refer Jack for a complete evaluation to rule in or out attention deficit hyperactivity disorder.

55. Shirley's objective is to get 90% of math problems correct on each test for eight consecutive weekly tests. On the graph below, the highest point = 90%. Based on this information, when evaluating the effectiveness of her instructional program, which is the most valid conclusion?

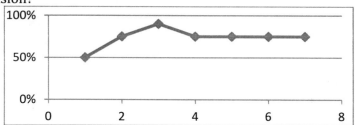

    a. Shirley's program needs re-evaluation because, being stuck at 75%, she may be unable to reach 90%.

    b. Shirley's program needs re-evaluation to become more challenging as she is consistently successful.

    c. Shirley's program needs re-evaluation because she has reached a plateau below objective criterion.

    d. Shirley's program needs no change as she has improved, is consistent, and simply needs more time.

56. Jim has mild cognitive impairment. On annual standardized tests, his scores averaged 20 percent below national averages this year and 35 percent below last year. He scored 90 percent correct on his performance-based assessments. He has met or exceeded his IEP goals to increase his criterion-referenced classroom test scores by an average of 10 percent over last year. Based on this information, which of the following is correct?

    a. Jim's instruction is effective because he is demonstrating progress and meeting goals

    b. Jim's instruction is not effective enough because he scored well below national norms

    c. Jim's instruction is effective within the school, but needs work for standardized tests

    d. Jim's instruction may or may not be effective; more information is needed to decide

57. Keith has a behavior disorder and expressive language deficits. His teacher wants to evaluate his progress toward his IEP goals for behavior. Which of the following would be the most appropriate method?

    a. Norm-referenced testing

    b. The teacher interviews Keith

    c. Observational assessment

    d. Curriculum-based testing

58. Which of the following is accurate about federal definitions of disability under the IDEA?

    a. Developmental delays are not considered as disabilities under the provisions of the IDEA.

    b. States and local educational agencies can include developmental delay to define disability.

    c. States can require local educational agencies to adopt/use the term "developmental delay."

    d. Local educational agencies can use developmental delay for eligibility without state adoption.

59. Which of the following is correct regarding the IEP process?

    a. A student's educational/behavioral difficulties will be documented and explained during pre-referral.

    b. Classroom accommodations and modifications' effectiveness are tested after eligibility determination.

    c. Different instructional interventions will be assessed for effectiveness after the IEP is implemented.

    d. The student's progress will be monitored only after the IEP has been developed and implemented.

60. Which of these is true about IDEA's procedural safeguards regarding informed parental consent?

    a. A public agency must give parents notice before evaluating a child, but does not need their consent.

    b. A public agency must both provide notice to and obtain informed consent from parents to evaluate.

    c. A public agency must obtain informed parent consent before providing services, but not to evaluate.

    d. A public agency must obtain informed parent consent for evaluation, but not for providing services.

61. According to the 2004 IDEA reauthorization, which is true of general requirements for IEP content?

    a. Since goals are annual, it is not necessary to include in the IEP when quarterly reports will be issued.

    b. The goals and objectives for the student's desired performance are included, but not current levels.

    c. The IEP must describe goals designed to meet the child's educational needs caused by the disability.

    d. The IEP must include a description of the quarterly academic and functional goals set for the student.

62. Which of the following major pieces of special education legislation occurred the earliest in time?

a. Changes to the federal law focusing on IEP, due process, and discipline provisions were authorized.

b. The public law regarding free appropriate public education to disabled children was named the IDEA.

c. Legislation guaranteed children aged 0–5 years with disabilities a free appropriate public education.

d. The Education for All Handicapped Children Acts (EHA) was passed by the U.S. federal government.

63. Several students with disabilities become extremely confused by the fragmentation of being "pulled out" of class to a resource room during one lesson and returning during another. Their IEP Committee finds it in their best interests to receive services from a special education teacher coming to their mainstreamed class. This role is designated as:

a. A resource teacher

b. An itinerant teacher

c. A consultant teacher

d. An inclusion teacher

64. A classroom includes one visually impaired student, two hearing-impaired students, three students with Down syndrome, and four with other intellectual disabilities. In addition to special education teachers, which of the following other professionals are most likely to be included in delivering special education services (excluding testing) to this group?

a. Physical therapist, occupational therapist, behavior specialist

b. Physical therapist, speech-language pathologist, orientation & mobility specialist, behavior specialist

c. Orientation and mobility specialist, physical therapist, school psychologist, audiologist

d. Audiologist, speech-language pathologist, orientation & mobility specialist, occupational therapist

65. With which of the following factors can collaborative teaching approaches present both advantages and disadvantages?

a. Larger class sizes caused by budget cuts and lack of physical space in the school

b. A significant proportion of students in the school receiving special education

c. The respective personalities and teaching styles of teachers collaborating

d. All of these factors can present both advantages and disadvantages.

66. You are a special education teacher. Which of the following is correct about how you should communicate with your students' general education teachers?

a. You should decide how often to communicate with them and inform them of this.

b. Give them a copy of each child's IEP, but discuss these only if there are problems.

c. Model for them how to deliver the differentiated instruction you have designed.

d. Homework is the province of general education teachers; do not tamper with it.

67. Which of the following activities reflects an inherent American mainstream cultural bias in the classroom?

    a. Students helping one another and/or working in groups to share information while taking a test

    b. Students seated independently, working quietly on a single task, only interacting with the teacher

    c. Students engaging in multiple activities at the same time and/or listening to music while working

    d. Students doing any or all of these things reflect the inherent bias of American mainstream culture.

68. Which of these is NOT a legal right of persons with intellectual disabilities?

    a. To be presumed legally incompetent for legal purposes

    b. To receive an education regardless of circumstances

    c. To have equal opportunities in employment

    d. To have equal opportunities in housing

69. Teddy's family has just moved from an isolated rural area. Teddy has never been taught reading, writing, or arithmetic. According to U.S. federal law, which of the following is true?

    a. Teddy may be determined to be functionally disabled.

    b. Teddy cannot be judged as disabled only by illiteracy.

    c. Teddy cannot receive remedial education for literacy.

    d. None of the above is true according to U. S. federal law.

70. Joaquin's family has recently immigrated to the USA from another country. He speaks only a little English. According to U.S. federal law, which of the following is true?

    a. Joaquin cannot be determined to be disabled due to his ESL status.

    b. Joaquin must only attend regular classes despite his language.

    c. Joaquin should be labeled as disabled to get him into ESL classes.

    d. Joaquin should go to a school emphasizing his first language.

71. Which of the following is correct regarding the 2004 reauthorization of IDEA relative to the No Child Left Behind Act?

    a. IDEA 2004 supersedes the provisions of No Child Left Behind.

    b. IDEA 2004 and No Child Left Behind are not directly related.

    c. IDEA 2004 contains regulations to align it better with NCLB.

    d. IDEA 2004 is another name for the No Child Left Behind Act.

72. The revised IDEA requires that if disproportionate numbers of students are identified as disabled, or those so identified are disproportionately placed in certain educational settings, allocated funds must be mainly used to:

    a. Reevaluate students to obtain different results.

    b. Give early intervention services to these students.

    c. Redistribute students to various education settings.

    d. Accomplish all of the educational goals outlined above.

73. By law, local educational agencies providing early intervention services must report what to state educational agencies each year?
    a. The number of students who received early intervention services
    b. The number of students who received special education services
    c. The number of students who received (a) and/or (b)
    d. None of the above

74. A recent provision added to the law allows for who/which of the following to request an initial evaluation to determine disability in a child?
    a. The child's parent
    b. A public agency
    c. Neither (a) nor (b)
    d. Either (a) or (b)

75. An addition made in recent years to laws for students with disabilities requires that evaluation procedures be administered:
    a. In the student's native language
    b. In American Sign Language
    c. In a nonverbal modality
    d. In any of these modes

Integrated Constructed Response Questions

76. Carly has been referred by her classroom teacher for evaluation. She is reading and writing at her grade level and generally achieves good grades. The only deficit in her performance appears to be her inability to produce the sound /r/ correctly. Being in fourth grade, she can be expected to have attained this norm by now. She exhibits hypersensitive reactions regarding this minor articulation problem: when asked to pronounce /r/, she often bursts into tears. Of more concern to the teacher is that Carly, while sweet and seeming eager to please and gain approval, is also very shy, quiet, and withdrawn. She does not initiate social interactions with her classmates, and she does not participate in group activities. She seems to worry excessively about many things. If confronted too assertively by teachers or other school personnel, she is likely to burst into tears. Identify three assessment instruments that would help to inform Carly's evaluation. Explain the value of each.

77. Alex has received a diagnosis of Oppositional Defiant Disorder. He is not aggressive toward other students, does not destroy property, and does not display violent behavior. However, he does tend to exhibit a negative attitude overall. He argues with teachers' directions and requests more often than not. He seems to need to prove to everybody that he does not need to comply with anything they want. Therefore, he is unable to cooperate either with adults or with his peers. This has the effect of isolating him, even though Alex seems to want social interaction. He just does not know how to engage in it in a positive way. His behavior is interfering with his academic performance. Moreover, it is preventing his having positive social interactions with others and making or keeping friends. Ultimately, Alex's behavior is also delaying the development of his social skills. Alex is receiving counseling outside of school from a child psychologist, and in-school counseling from the school psychologist. In addition to these, his IEP specifies classroom management methods. Identify three classroom management techniques that can help Alex in school. Explain the value of each.

78. Consider the scenario that you are a special education teacher who is going to be working collaboratively in a middle school with the general education teachers of the mainstreamed classrooms attended by the students in your caseload. All of your students, of course, have IEPs. In addition, several of the students in your caseload have Behavior Management Plans. Several of your students have specific learning disabilities with reading. Identify four things you can do to establish enhanced communication, cooperation, and collaboration with your students' general education classroom teachers. Explain the value of each.

Answers and Explanations

1. D: According to Piaget and cognitive-developmental theory, when a child can mentally reverse what has been done—e.g., knowing liquid poured into a differently shaped container is still the same amount as before (conservation of volume), or a ball of clay rolled into a "snake" is the same amount—s/he has attained reversibility, a key feature of the Formal Operations stage. Object permanence (A), i.e., knowing things/people still exist when out of sight, develops during infancy in the Sensorimotor stage. Egocentrism (B), i.e., thinking everything revolves around oneself, is characteristic of toddlers in the Preoperational stage. Pretend play (C) also emerges during this period, indicating understanding of symbolic representation.

2. A: Positive reinforcement is presenting something the individual likes immediately following his/her emission of a desired behavior. When the behavior is rewarded, the individual is more likely to repeat it. Negative reinforcement (B) is removing something the individual dislikes following the desired behavior. Positive punishment (C) is presenting something the individual dislikes following an undesired behavior. Response extinction (D) is giving neither reward nor punishment to a behavior but ignoring it. If the behavior was attention-seeking, ignoring will eventually extinguish it. Positive reinforcement has proven more effective than any of these others.

3. C: The discomfort Cara feels over two conflicting ideas has been dubbed Cognitive Dissonance by Leon Festinger. His theory posits that the need to resolve this discomfort motivates our choices/actions. Attribution Theory (A) posits that we attribute causes to events—external causes like bad luck or biased teachers to failures, and internal causes like ability or effort to successes. Expectancy Theory (B) finds we are motivated by things we want that we expect we can attain. Extrinsic Motivation (D) Theory explains how we are motivated by environmental rewards in contrast to gratifying internal needs.

4. B: Historically, only IQ scores (A) were considered for diagnosing intellectual disabilities. However, this has changed, and today both intellectual and adaptive functioning (C) are examined; a diagnosis of intellectual disabilities includes deficits in both areas. Academic achievement deficits (D) do not determine intellectual disabilities: these can be caused by many other things, e.g., ADHD; vision/hearing impairment; autism; mental illness; lack of motivation, etc.

5. A: A prominent characteristic of autism is difficulty starting and continuing conversations, friendships, and other social interactions due to difficulty noticing and understanding others' emotional and social cues. Difficulty focusing and maintaining attention on nonsocial activities (B) and/or sitting still and staying quiet (D) are more characteristic of ADHD but are not generally problems for autistic students, who often focus exclusively on one solitary activity for long periods. Difficulty understanding abstract ideas (C) is more characteristic of intellectual disabilities. Autistic students without intellectual disabilities are more likely to have emotional/social impairments than intellectual ones.

6. C: According to research (e.g. Heller, UI Chicago, 2010), the generation that has received school services mandated by the IDEA has accordingly come to expect more support throughout life, including support for being able to grow older at home. This support is more necessary because life expectancies for the developmentally disabled have increased

similarly to those for others (A). Although the majority of DD adults live with their families, only roughly 5% of funding for DD is used for family support (B). Research finds adults with DDs are more likely to develop chronic health problems (D).

7. D: Disproportionate representation of CLD students in special education programs can and does exist as overidentification of CLD students as having DDs (A); some CLD groups' being categorized as emotionally disturbed or intellectually disabled in higher proportions (B) than others; and within special education programs, higher proportions of CLD students being placed in more restrictive (C) or segregated programs than others are.

8. B: Cathy cannot communicate orally with caregivers due to her deafness. She is also less likely to initiate social interactions with caregivers due to her autism. Rather than serving no purpose (A), the self-injurious behavior she exhibits when in physical distress serves the purpose of attempting to communicate her distress and need for the relief caregivers can provide. Her coexisting conditions make this behavior more likely; however, the behavior is not caused by any one of them, (C) or (D).

9. A: The more the parents focus their anxiety and worry on a child with an impairment, the more the child in turn focuses anxiety and worry on the parents. The parents' greater focus of anxiety on one child decreases that child's differentiation of self from the family rather than increasing it (B). The child with the disability becomes more reactive than his/her siblings to parental expectations, needs, and attitudes, not less (C). The child with a disability is more likely to internalize or externalize family tensions, not less (D).

10. C: Not only does federal law mandate inclusion of DD students in the least restrictive educational programs wherein they can participate, which includes access to academically rigorous programs (D) where applicable; but moreover, research finds that realistically high teacher expectations encourage DD students to perform better rather than only frustrating them (B). The law also mandates that students with DDs do receive reasonable accommodations (A) they need to enable their educational participation.

11. D: Down syndrome, which is caused by the presence of an extra chromosome, is the most frequent cause of intellectual disabilities in infancy.

12. C: The development of moral realism is basically the comprehension that morality is fixed rather than subjective.

13. C: Approximately 2 to 3% of the population is classified as intellectually disabled and there are approximately 7 million intellectually disabled individuals in the United States.

14. A: The physical and behavioral symptoms of learning disability vary widely so the most common observation made by teachers is that capable students are not achieving their potential.

15. B: Rubella is extremely contagious and is usually transmitted through mucus. Rubella may cause deafness, intellectual disabilities, and/or cataracts, but it does not cause scoliosis.

16. A: Judy's action reflects a need for remediation in the area of affective behavior (a), which includes interpersonal skills, social interactions, and emotional intelligence. Self-esteem issues (b) may or may not be a part of Judy's needs, but this choice is not directly

related to the behavior described. The example does not give information related to this choice. The same is true of self-concept issues (c). The question does state that Judy has good expressive verbal skills. Therefore, a deficit in communication (d) is probably not the reason for her physical aggression. Her aggression is more related to emotional self-regulation and behavior control.

17. D: Answer choices (a), (b), and (c) are included in IDEA's definition of intellectual disabilities, making (d) the correct answer. The Individuals with Disabilities Education Act (IDEA) defines intellectual disabilities as having general intellectual functioning that is significantly below average. This occurs concurrently with deficits in adaptive behavior (a). These deficits manifest during the developmental period (c) (i.e. before 18 years of age) and adversely affect the child's educational performance (b).

18. C: The WISC-IV (c) is not primarily* an assessment of adaptive skills. Rather, it is primarily an IQ test. The Wechsler Intelligence Scales for Children, Fourth Edition (WISC-IV) consists of a number of subscales testing different intellectual functions such as verbal comprehension, perceptual reasoning, working memory, and processing speed. These are all cognitive functions. *(Note: AAIDD's definition of intellectual disabilities, unlike IDEA's, includes receptive language, which incorporates verbal comprehension as a "conceptual" adaptive skill under its conceptual, social, and practical divisions of adaptive skills. However, the primary purpose of the Wechsler Scales is to test intellectual abilities.) The Walker-McConnell (a) Scales of Social Competence and School Adjustment are designed to assess adaptive functioning in the area of social skills. The Vineland (b) Adaptive Behavior Scales, as the full name suggests, are used to assess adaptive behaviors in people of all ages. Areas assessed include communication, daily living skills, socialization, motor skills, and an optional maladaptive behavior index. The SSRS (d) is the Social Skills Rating System. It gives measurements of positive social behaviors (including cooperation, empathy, assertion, self-control, and responsibility) and problem behaviors (including externalizing problems, internalizing problems, and hyperactivity). The SSRS also includes an academic competence scale, which is a brief measure of general cognitive functioning, performance in reading and math, and motivation and parental support. However, the primary purpose of the SSRS, as its name indicates, is to assess social skills, which are considered adaptive skills.

19. A: The majority of people with intellectual disabilities (an estimated 87%) have mild intellectual disabilities (a). The remaining 13% is made up of people with moderate (b), severe (c), and profound (d) intellectual disabilities. People with mild levels of intellectual disabilities have IQ scores above 50-55. Their childhood development may be only a bit slower than normal, and they may not be identified with intellectual disabilities until they reach school. Many adults with mild intellectual disabilities can live autonomously and hold down jobs. People may know them and, if they do not know of the diagnosis, not be aware that they have intellectual disabilities.

20. D: Time stands for Time-based, i.e., the objective should specify in what length of time, or by what point in time, it is to be attained. M stands not for Memorable (A), but Measurable: the objective must be something that can be objectively measured or quantified. A stands not for Activities (B), but Appropriate: the objective should be suitable to the purpose the activity is intended to accomplish. R stands not for Resources (C), but Realistic: the objective should be possible to achieve with the instructional experience and resources available.

21. C: Three components of an effective lesson plan included under Instructional Procedures are Opening (A), i.e., getting students interested, activating their existing knowledge, and connecting the new material to it; Engagement (B), i.e., facilitating and monitoring active and reflective student learning and discourse and asking specific questions to help students take risks and develop deeper understanding; and Closure (C), i.e., highlighting main lesson points for student comprehension; giving students opportunities to share their comprehension; and asking questions to obtain meaningful student feedback. Assessment (C) is not an instructional procedure but a separate section covering how you evaluate student learning, aligned with lesson objectives.

22. D: A good lesson plan should specify both which formative (B), i.e., ongoing, and summative (A), i.e., overall, assessments will be used to evaluate what students learn from the lesson—not just one or the other. Assessments should be congruent with the plan's learning objectives. The lesson plan should always include, not exclude (C) what types of formative and summative assessments will measure student learning.

23. B: This objective specifies what John should be able to do through the lesson; it is measurable by specifying a minimum score on all appropriate assessments indicated in the lesson plan; and it specifies by what time he should have achieved this. (A) does not specify how to measure or assess John's reading ability or comprehension, or any time frame. (C) not only fails to specify these things, but moreover is unrealistic in dictating 100%. (D) not only fails to specify measurability; it moreover states only what activity John will complete, but not what he should learn and be able to do through completing it.

24. A: Speech-to-text software can convert the teacher's spoken lessons, lectures, and directions to a format the hearing-impaired student can read visually. Text-to-speech software (B), text magnification (C), and large print (D) are all more suited to providing access to the curriculum for a student who is blind or visually impaired.

25. D: The IDEA requires that disabled students receiving special education services be given access to the general education curriculum, that they also be actively involved in it (B), and moreover that they make progress in it (C). General education classrooms' becoming more inclusive does NOT automatically give disabled students more access to the general curriculum (A); instead, it requires educators to provide more strategies and means for disabled students to gain access to it.

26. C: Expert educators recommend creating a "meeting" area big enough for all students in the class to gather for participating in large group activities, engaging in discussions, and developing their social skills. Too many bright colors and clutter (A) can cause sensory overload and/or distractions for disabled (and nondisabled) students. Storing class materials on high shelves (B) makes them inaccessible to wheelchair-bound, physically disabled, and smaller students. Teachers also recommend placing students' desks in small groups rather than far apart (D): grouping desks gives students more opportunities for learning collaboration, cooperation, and discussion.

27. A: Janice's behavior has a clear purpose: to get the teacher's attention when she needs help. Teaching her a more acceptable replacement behavior, i.e., raising her hand/waving her arm, will fulfill the same purpose less disruptively. Punishment (B) of undesired behaviors has proven less effective than positive reinforcement of more desired behaviors; moreover, it does not provide an alternative for meeting Janice's need. Extinction through

ignoring (C) also provides no replacement behavior; allows continuing, aggravated disruption meanwhile; and would teach Janice NOT to ask for needed help. Giving constant attention (D) is simply impracticable in a classroom with other students; and, even if possible, would give Janice unrealistic expectations and worse behaviors.

28. B: The first step is to determine what function(s) or purpose(s) the behaviors serve by conducting a functional behavior analysis (FBA). Students should never be referred for special education without first trying classroom interventions, determined through the FBA; also, a conduct or behavior disorder should not be assumed if it has not been diagnosed after thorough evaluation (A). Moving the student to a separate classroom (C) is also inappropriate. Even after the FBA, classroom interventions, referral if indicated, evaluation, diagnosis, and placement in special education if indicated, the least restrictive environment as dictated by law is more likely to be inclusive than segregated. Recommending special school placement to parents (D) is also premature and inappropriate.

29. B: Purposefully building networks in the classroom can enable supportive and meaningful relationships among teachers and students. Starting class the first day with a combination of paired, small-group, and whole-class activities helps students get acquainted; providing continuing opportunities to connect with others with whom they interact less often affords contacts, skills, and friendships to students and staff beyond their immediate communities. One example of building self-esteem and self-efficacy (A) is giving students initial experiences of success. Some examples of positive nonverbal communication (C) include making eye contact, smiling, and including gestures to enliven teaching style. Motivating students by engaging their active participation (D) includes asking students questions more than telling them things; showing enthusiasm for teaching content; and building upon students' strengths and interests.
progresses.

30. D: Answers (a), (b), and (c) are all alternative placements identified in IDEA's definition, making (d) the correct answer. Instruction in special classes, in special schools (a), in regular schools (b), in hospitals (c), in institutions, and in the home are all included as placements on the continuum of alternative placements required by law to meet the needs of students requiring special education services.

31. C: Mainstreamed instruction (c) is not defined as a supplementary service by IDEA. Placing students with intellectual disabilities in regular classes, or mainstreaming, is the least restrictive service delivery model of all options under the Least Restrictive Environment provision of the law. When students needing special education are placed in regular classrooms, they are receiving the same school placement as students without special education needs, so mainstreaming is not a supplementary service. Instruction in a resource room (a) is a supplementary service, as resource rooms are designated for special education students. Instruction by itinerant staff (b) is a supplementary service. Some personnel in the special education field, such as speech-language pathologists, audiologists, physical and occupational therapists, and special education teachers, may travel among schools, homes, hospitals, or other educational settings to deliver services on a periodic basis rather than being at one location full-time. These are typically not teachers in regular classrooms. Since (c) is not defined as a supplementary service but (a) and (b) are, answer (d) is incorrect.

32. A: The psychometric perspective on education views differences in individual student performance as reflections of how much of an ability or skill each student has. In contrast, the developmental perspective, not the psychometric (B), views these differences as reflecting each student's rate of intellectual growth. Psychometric approaches, not developmental (C), seek to match students with other students according to ability level. Developmental approaches, not psychometric (D), seek to match curricula with students' emerging intellectual skills.

33. C: Developmental psychologists find the learning process inextricable from the content being learned in that the content dictates the level of problem-solving strategies applied by the learner. In contrast, psychometrically-oriented educators find the learning process determined by principles (A); and composed of skills acquisition, separately from the content being learned (B). Additionally, psychometric educators assume that skills learned automatically transfer to other subjects, whereas developmental educators assume little or no spontaneous transfer (D), finding active learning necessary to achieve generalization.

34. D: Students with learning disabilities often avoid asking questions in large classes/groups. Teachers can encourage them to take risks by giving cues that support their asking "wh-" questions. Pairing students to discuss teacher questions (A) is a good strategy to engage all LD students in a large class. Asking LD students to summarize main lesson points (B) is a good strategy to discern whether they understand these, and reviewing benefits all students. Having LD students complete reminder worksheets at the end of the lesson (C) is a good strategy to see what they have learned, what they enjoyed, and what else they know about the subject.

35. B: Research studies show that 1:1 instruction is highly effective with students who are failing to learn to read. This is a valid argument for providing such instruction. The other answer choices are all examples of factors that make 1:1 instruction difficult or impossible: overly large caseloads (A); increasing demands for collaborative teaching (C), decreasing time for direct instruction; and growing paperwork (D), which improves service documentation but interferes with service implementation.

36. A: Educators and researchers working with DD students find similarities between tasks and settings during both instruction and application facilitate transfer. They also find the traditional three-stage hierarchy of skill acquisition, fluency, and transfer (B) is NOT as effective as supporting transfer from the beginning of instruction. Another factor facilitating transfer is the student's ability to discriminate (C) when/when NOT to apply a learned skill. Transfer and maintenance are additionally supported by practicing relevant basic skills until these become automatic (D): students must be fluent in foundations to attain higher learning levels.

37. B: Most models of research-based interventions for individual students include differentiated instruction for all students—those performing both below and above grade level, students learning English, those with developmental disabilities, etc. Typical models first establish school-wide or district-wide emotional, social, and behavioral supports (A), adding progressively more intensive individual interventions for students not succeeding with the general supports (commonly through a 3-tier system). Typically, students stay in general classrooms (C), even when also receiving additional, more individualized/intensive instruction. Progress monitoring is continual, including frequent, brief assessments throughout interventions (D).

38. C: Since he has never directly or indirectly experienced paying work, employment training is the most important supplemental/functional curriculum for Stan to become more independent. His ability to perform all self-care suggests he does not need training in ADLs (A) as much as job training. His ability to count money and make change and understand common signs suggests he does not need as much training in functional academics (B) as in employment skills. Hence, not all these are equally needed (D).

39. D: A word processor with voice output can help the student whose hearing impairment makes speech more difficult and less clear; the student with other communication deficits impeding expressive language and/or speech; the student with cognitive deficits impeding speech-language development; and, especially with prediction as well as voice output, the student with fine-motor skills deficits impeding typing. The touch screen (A) would benefit students with fine-motor skills deficits and cognitive deficits more than the others. Classroom amplification (B) would help the hearing-impaired student, but not others. Large print/books on tape (C) would benefit students with visual impairments and/or cognitive deficits more than the others.

40. C: The best way to achieve a smooth transition is for Sue to continue her educational program half of the time and begin employment the other half, but accompanied by a job coach, not alone (B), since she needs prompting and supervision to perform work tasks. Remaining at school only while refocusing instruction on job tasks and counseling (A) will not give her workplace exposure or experience to adjust to the new setting. Switching abruptly from school to job, with (D) or without (B) supervision, omits any transitional experiences, which should include and bridge both settings.

41. B: Many instructional models use a progressively tiered system. The first tier typically consists of general education classroom core instruction and school-wide (or school system/district-wide) behavioral supports, which all students receive as a way to prevent school problems before they start. Students not succeeding receive second-tier, short-term targeted interventions (A). Those whom this does not help then receive third-tier, more intensive, more individualized interventions (C). Only if the student continues to fail with these do educators refer them for Special Education evaluation (D).

42. D: In Lev Vygotsky's social-cognitive theory, the concept of scaffolding refers to support that is provided to learners (by parents, teachers, other adults, peers, etc.) when they need it to learn a task or skill, and which is gradually withdrawn as the learner becomes more able to perform that task or skill independently. It is a form of support for all learners, not just special needs children, and it is not always there (B), but is decreased little by little corresponding to the learner's progress. It is not a structural framework for a lesson (A) or for social interactions (C).

43. C: The change that will most likely address the issue described in the question is creating a transition from every activity to the next (b). Students with intellectual disabilities and other developmental disabilities such as autism frequently have difficulty with abrupt changes and making transitions. Giving advance notice of changes and building in bridges between events or activities can help students adjust. Making all activities shorter (a) would help if students were demonstrating behavior problems part of the way through an activity, their attention wandered, or they exhibited fatigue during the activity. These would all indicate that the activity might be too long. These students, however, only

display problem behaviors when switching activities. Scheduling rest breaks is important, but a break after every single activity (b) could be excessive, especially if there are many short activities. Giving too many breaks too frequently could encourage off-task behavior, reinforce attentional deficits, and even prohibit sufficient periods of actual learning. Asking for each student to have a behavior management program (d) is inappropriate since they all demonstrate very good behavior during activities.

44. A: With students who have disabilities, the time to introduce each career development stage depends more on the individual student's developmental level, which often is not commensurate with the student's grade level (B) or chronological age (D) in some or all domains. While the student's experiential level (C) is important for selecting instructional materials and methods, the developmental level has more impact on whether a student will be able to learn the skills acquired in each stage.

45. A: Setting up a token economy (a) is most effective for this cognitive level. Receiving concrete rewards for accomplishing target tasks is reinforcing, and does not require the ability to think abstractly. Having the student make checklists (b) would be expecting too much of an individual functioning at this level. If a teacher or staff person made up a checklist for him, he could check off each item as he completed it. This could be tied in with a token system if, for example, he received a reward for checking off all items in the morning routine. He could also be given a gold star/sticker to put on the checklist for each item as mini-reinforcements, and a larger reward could be given after a star had been placed in all items that are part of a routine. Playing a DVD on self-care (c) would not be effective with this student as he is not likely to apply what he sees to his own behaviors. People at this cognitive level (as well as others) learn more successfully by doing than by observing. Giving ongoing verbal prompts (d) will not lead to independence. Prompts will likely be needed to get him to initiate each task, but these should be phased out as he progresses.

46. A: The TOWL is an evidence-based assessment of a student's basic writing skills because its results are norm-referenced and supported by experimental research results. The other choices are all equally effective methods of assessing basic student writing. However, "evidence-based" is less descriptive of these because they rely on individual teacher methods and/or individual student writing samples, but they are not proven by evidence from research studies and do not compare student results to those of normative student sample groups.

47. D: The XBA approach can enhance comprehensiveness by allowing use of subtests from different test instruments focusing on the same cognitive and/or academic area(s). It also enhances selectivity and depth by allowing selection from different batteries of subtests most relevant to the student's presenting difficulties. Researchers have found this approach useful for assessing reading and writing disorders, but this is not its sole or primary use; and this approach is evidence-based (A), as research evidence supports its application. The XBA approach assesses across domains of both academic (B) and intellectual (C) performance.

48. B: The Peabody Picture Vocabulary Test (PPVT) tests vocabulary knowledge, and is often used as part of a battery for testing overall intelligence, through receptive language only. The only expressive response by the student is gestural, i.e., pointing at which one of several presented pictures matches a word read aloud by the tester. The other IQ measures

listed all include various subscales, many of which require the student to respond using speech.

49. C: The Wechsler Individual Achievement Test (WIAT) requires both written and oral verbal responses on many of its subtests. The UNIT (A) is the Universal Nonverbal Intelligence Test. The TONI (B) is the Test of Nonverbal Intelligence. The Raven (D) Progressive Matrices is a nonverbal intelligence test that requires the student to identify patterns in visual stimuli. Except for the WIAT, the others are intelligence measures that are not affected by verbal ability or the lack of it.

50. A: The Leiter International Performance Scale is a completely nonverbal test. It is useful for testing intelligence in nonverbal/verbally limited autistic, ESL/ELL/non-English-speaking, cognitively impaired, developmentally delayed, deaf/hearing-impaired, speech-impaired, and motor-impaired students. Subscales of the Wechsler Intelligence Scales for Children (B) require receptive verbal understanding and expressive verbal ability. The Woodcock-Johnson (C) Tests of Cognitive Abilities also include subtests requiring verbal responses; in fact, one of its three "broad cognitive areas" is Verbal Ability. The Reynolds Intellectual Assessment Scales (D) measure both nonverbal and verbal intelligence.

51. B: The FSIQ stands for Full Scale IQ. It is the sum of the test's four index scores: the Verbal Comprehension Index (VCI), from the Similarities, Comprehension, and Vocabulary subtests; the Perceptual Reasoning Index (PRI), using the Matrix Reasoning, Picture Concepts, and Block Design subtests; the Working Memory Index (WMI), from the Letter-Number Sequencing and Digit Span subtests; and the Processing Speed Index (PSI), from the Coding and Symbol Search subtests. FSIQ gives a global IQ score. It is not the average of all subtest scores (A) or a separate unrelated score (C). Wechsler's tests do use FSIQ (D).

52. C: Cognitive or intellectual functioning is the student's intelligence, as reflected by scores from IQ testing; adaptive functioning is the student's ability to perform the activities of daily living (ADL) independently. Historically, intelligence was measured only by IQ scores; today, both intellectual functioning and adaptive functioning are included. Intellectual and adaptive functioning do not equate to abstract and concrete thinking (B). Choices (A) and (D) are basically the same.

53. D: These are all applications of evaluation results. All students determined eligible for Special Education services must have an IEP. In writing it, educators must include the student's Present Level of Functioning (A). To decide what the student needs to learn, by when, and how it will be measured, educators must establish baseline scores; retesting with the same instruments after a period of intervention and comparing scores will show if the intervention is effective (B) if scores improve. To make developmentally appropriate placement decisions, educators must know at what levels the student currently performs (C).

54. D: The characteristics described are most similar to the symptoms of attention deficit hyperactivity disorder (ADHD). They do not suggest a major mental illness (A). Jack should only have a behavior management program written for him (B) after receiving a full evaluation and diagnosis, and then only after less restrictive classroom interventions are tried sufficiently but fail. A disorder like ADHD will not respond to disciplinary measures (C). If ADHD is Jack's diagnosis as test results suggest, he may benefit from medication and

will need a carefully structured program of behavior modification and adaptive instructional strategies.

55. C: Shirley's program should be re-evaluated because her objective criterion is 90%, but she has scored 75% for four tests in a row. It is not valid to assume she may be unable to reach 90% (A) because she already reached 90% once (point 3). While her last four scores were consistent, they cannot be considered successful (B) because they do not meet the objective criterion. It cannot be assumed she simply needs more time (D), because her scores initially improved but then fell and have not changed over four tests. Her program should be adjusted to enable her to progress to and maintain 90%.

56. A: Jim's instruction can be considered quite effective, as he has not only scored 90 percent on classroom performance assessments and met or surpassed his IEP goals, but he has also increased his score on national norm-referenced standardized tests by 15 percent in a year. Scoring 20 percent below national norms does not indicate that his instruction is not effective enough (B) because (1) norm-referenced tests are not useful for determining instructional effectiveness, as state and local teaching practices vary too much for the broad range of content on these tests to apply; and (2) because Jim has mild cognitive impairment and may or may not ever score equally with national averages. Because norm-referenced tests do not indicate instructional effectiveness, working on his instruction just to raise his scores on these tests (C) is unnecessary. More information is not needed (D) to know that he is demonstrating progress, so his instructional program must be working.

57. C: Any kind of observational assessment will involve direct observation of Keith's behavior, which is what the teacher wants to evaluate. If the teacher uses the same recording methods as for behavioral baseline measures, comparing current results to baseline can indicate Keith's progress. Norm-referenced tests (A) are standardized tests and typically measure academic achievement, not behavior. Interviewing Keith (B) is contraindicated because he has expressive language deficits and may have difficulty responding, and also because observing what the student does is more accurate than asking the student to describe his own behavior. Curriculum-based testing (D) connects assessment to instruction. While behavioral interventions have probably been incorporated during Keith's classroom instruction, curriculum-based assessments are related to curriculum content areas, not behavioral issues.

58. B: The IDEA provides that with children aged 3 through 9 years, states and local educational agencies (LEAs) can include the term "developmental delay" in their definition of a "child with a disability" eligible for Special Education services. Thus, DDs are considered disabilities (A) under these conditions. The IDEA also stipulates that a state may NOT require LEAs to adopt and/or use the term "developmental delay" (C). Moreover, if a state does not adopt this term, its LEAs may NOT independently use it to determine eligibility for Special Education services under the IDEA (D).

59. A: Documenting and explaining a student's educational/behavioral difficulties occur during the pre-referral stage of the IEP process. Classroom accommodations and modifications are tested for effectiveness NOT after determining eligibility (B) for Special Education services, but during pre-referral. The effectiveness of different instructional interventions is assessed NOT after IEP implementation (C) but during pre-referral. Progress monitoring is done NOT only after IEP implementation (D) but also during pre-

referral. The IEP process steps are: Pre-referral, referral, identification, eligibility, IEP development, IEP implementation, and evaluation and reviews.

60. B: The federal IDEA's procedural safeguards specify that public agencies must both provide notice to parents (A), and obtain their informed consent (C), both before evaluating a child to determine eligibility for special education services and before providing such services (D) to the child if s/he is determined eligible through the evaluation.

61. C: The revised general IDEA 2004 requirements for IEP content include the IEP state annual, not quarterly (D), goals for the student that are measurable, and are designed to meet the student's educational needs resulting from the disability. The IDEA requires that IEPs always contain a statement of the student's present levels of academic and functional performance (B). Although the IDEA requires annual IEP goals, it also requires IEPs to indicate when quarterly or other periodic reports will be issued, so this information must be included (A).

62. D: The EHA (PL 94-142) was passed in 1975. In 1986, it was amended to include a free appropriate public education (FAPE) to children with disabilities aged 3 to 5 years; Early Intervention Programs (EIP) for children aged 0 to 2 years; and Individualized Family Service Plans (IFSP) for families of infants/toddlers with disabilities (C). EHA was amended again in 1990, changing its name to the Individuals with Disabilities Education Act (IDEA) (B). The IDEA was amended again in 1997 to include: access to general curriculum as part of the Least Restrictive Environment (LRE); orientation and mobility services under related services; and Assistive Technology Devices and Services considered in all IEPs. It was reauthorized again in 2004 with changes focusing on its IEP, due process, and discipline provisions (A).

63. C: A consultant teacher works in the mainstreamed classroom with students having disabilities. A resource teacher (A) works with students having disabilities in a resource room where all students have disabilities. An itinerant teacher (B) visits multiple schools and/or districts. An inclusion teacher (D) team-teaches with a general education teacher in an inclusion class, i.e., a mainstreamed class containing both disabled and nondisabled students.

64. D: The audiologist is likely to deliver services to the hearing-impaired students. The SLP is likely to deliver services to both the hearing-impaired students and those with Down syndrome. The O&M specialist is likely to serve the visually impaired student. The OT is likely to serve the intellectually disabled and/or any students with poor fine motor control, common in this population. The PT [(A), (B), and (C)] would serve students with poor gross motor control, not identified here. Excluding testing as specified, the school psychologist and behavior specialist [(A), (B), and (C)] are less likely to serve this group as no emotional, social, or behavioral problems are identified.

65. D: All of these factors can be helped or harmed by collaborative teaching approaches. On one hand, two team-teachers can cut in half the burden of a large class size (A) that one teacher would have. On the other hand, school administrators may view this halved burden as license to have even larger classes. Even for two teachers, a class of 40 rather than 20 or even 30 is harder to manage. With team-teaching, one teacher can be a special education teacher, so more students in each class get these services than if the teacher moves among classes—an advantage. But if special education students are grouped in one class, inclusion

is sacrificed—a disadvantage (B). Teacher personalities and teaching styles (C) are advantages if they are similar or complementary; they are disadvantages if they clash.

66. C: Do not expect the general education teachers to know how to deliver the differentiated instruction you have designed. Experts recommend modeling to show them how, and coaching them in adapting their teaching for your special ed. students. They also advise starting by asking, not telling (A), general ed. teachers how often to communicate, and what they need to succeed. You should give teachers copies of each child's IEP, but also make appointments to review IEP goals and specialized instruction with them (B). Despite resistance, you should also adapt homework for your special ed. students (D). For example, ask how long teachers expect students to spend nightly on homework, and devise alternative/adapted homework that practices the indicated skills but only takes each student the time specified.

67. B: The mainstream culture in America is biased toward having students in classrooms stay independently seated, quiet, working on only one task at a time, and interacting only with the teacher. However, the diverse cultural backgrounds of many students in America differ: many cultures are not individualist like the mainstream, but collectivist; helping each other and working in groups (A) are frowned on by teachers but are more natural to these students. African-American and other cultures permit multiple activities or working with music (C) at home, yet these are often penalized at school.

68. A: It is not a legal right of persons with intellectual disabilities to be presumed incompetent for legal purposes (a). It is the right of persons with intellectual disabilities to be presumed legally competent until or unless adjudicated by a court of law as incompetent. In addition to this right, state and federal laws give people with intellectual disabilities the right to education, regardless of the level of intellectual disabilities, the person's age, the nature of the person's disability, or the person's residence (b); the right to equal employment opportunities (c), including candidacy for employment based on abilities related to jobs rather than exclusion due only to intellectual disabilities diagnosis; and the right to equal housing opportunities (d), which includes not being discriminated against in housing because of a diagnosis of intellectual disabilities.

69. B: According to U.S. federal law, Teddy cannot be judged as disabled solely because he is illiterate (b). IDEA stipulates that a student "....must not be determined to be a child with a disability under 34 CFR Part 300 if the determinant factor...is lack of appropriate instruction in reading...as defined in...the ESEA [or]...in math...." The ESEA is the Elementary and Secondary Education Act of 1965. Title I of this act was amended in 2001 by the No Child Left Behind Act, which is also referred to in IDEA documents as the ESEA. Teddy may not be determined to be functionally disabled (a). It is not true that he cannot receive remedial education for his illiteracy (c). It is only true that he cannot be classified as having a disability because of it. He can still receive remedial teaching that will eventually bring his skills up to the appropriate age/grade level. Since (b) is correct, answer (d) is incorrect.

70. A: By U.S. federal law, Joaquin cannot be determined to be disabled due to his ESL status (a). IDEA 2004 states that in addition to lack of instruction in reading or math, a student "....must not be determined to be a child with a disability...if the determinant factor...is...limited English proficiency." It is not true that Joaquin must only attend regular classes (b); there are classes and teachers for ESL (English as a Second Language) and ELL

(English Language Learners) students in America. Depending on students' levels of comprehension and expression in English and the individual school's resources, they may receive ESL instruction part of the day and attend regular classrooms part of the day; or they may have all of their instruction from ESL or ELL teachers until they achieve greater English proficiency. Joaquin should not be classified as disabled to get him into ESL classes (c). This is illegal as well as unnecessary. A student cannot and need not be determined disabled for this purpose. Joaquin should not go to a school emphasizing his first language (d) unless he and his parents do not want him to learn English, which would prevent his assimilation into the predominant society and culture.

71. C: IDEA 2004 includes regulations that align this law more closely with the No Child Left Behind Act (c). It does not supersede the provisions of NCLB (a). It is not true that these laws are not directly related (b). They were always related in that many of their definitions and topics overlap. Furthermore, they became more closely related when IDEA was revised in 2004. Those who prepared the revised version of IDEA made certain that its regulations correlated more closely with definitions in NCLB, which was signed into law in 2001. The new regulations sought to avoid conflict by increasing the compatibility of these two laws, which are not different names for the same law (d), but are two related yet distinct acts.

72. B: IDEA's new regulations require that if disabled students are overidentified or overplaced in certain settings, the maximal funds allowed must be used to give early intervention services to these students (b). The law does not require re-evaluating such students to get different results (a). Reevaluation should only be done if the original results are suspected of being invalid, and must never be done with the intention of altering or falsifying the students' performance. The law does not dictate redistribution of students to various educational settings (c), which could violate district regulations, require alternative transportation, and inconvenience students and families. It does dictate early intervention for overidentified or overplaced students. The law does not direct the distribution of funds for all of these purposes (d), as only one (b) is mandated by the act.

73. C: Revisions to the law require annual reporting by local educational agencies (LEAs) to their state educational agencies (SEAs) of the number of students who received early intervention services (a) and the number of students who received special education services (b) in the past two years. Therefore, (c) is the correct answer. Since (c) is correct, answer (d) is incorrect.

74. D: The child's parent(s) (a) OR a public agency (b)—not both—may request an initial evaluation of a child to determine whether the child has a disability [IDEA - 34 CFR 300.301(b)] [20 U.S.C. 1414(a)(1)(B)], making (d) the correct answer. Because (d) is correct, answer (c) is incorrect.

75. D: Legally, administration of evaluations may be required in any of the modes identified in (a), (b), or (c) depending on the individual student, making (d) the correct answer. An addition to the law in recent years requires that administration of evaluation procedures be in whatever form "....most likely to yield the most accurate information....on what the child knows and can do academically, developmentally, and functionally, unless it is clearly not feasible to provide or administer." [34 CFR 300.304(c)(1)(ii)] [20 U.S.C. 1414(b)(3)(A)(ii)] In other words, if the student is not a native speaker of English, evaluations should be administered in the student's native language (a). If a deaf student uses American Sign Language to communicate, evaluations should be administered using ASL (b). If a student is

completely nonverbal both receptively and expressively, appropriate evaluation instruments such as the Leiter International Performance Scale or Raven's Progressive Matrices that allow for nonverbal assessment should be used. Assessment and instruction techniques for students with special needs that do not use the modality or form of the student's usual communication also violate the law that states such students must not be treated prejudicially or be discriminated against.

Integrated Constructed Response Questions

76. Three assessment instruments:
    (1) Beck Depression Inventory
    (2) Beck Anxiety Inventory
    (3) Speech pathology evaluation

Explanations of value:
    (1) The Beck Depression Inventory is simply and quickly administered. Carly's withdrawn behavior, avoidance of social interactions, and hypersensitivity could be symptoms of depression. This instrument will help both identify the condition and indicate whether further psychological evaluation is needed.
    (2) The observations that Carly seems to worry excessively over many things, is eager to please and gain approval, and her hypersensitive reactions to confrontation or pressure warrant completing the Beck Anxiety Inventory. It is not uncommon for anxiety to accompany depression and vice versa. Completing both inventories by the same author for both emotional disorders will inform how serious the problems may be and the need for further psychological evaluation.
    (3) Since Carly has one phoneme she is not producing correctly by the usual age norm, and moreover since her emotional overreactions associated with this minor articulation defect indicate she feels traumatized by it, she will benefit from evaluation by a speech-language pathologist, who can then design therapy to help her correct her articulation. The SLP may also work with the psychologist or behavior specialist for counseling. However, regardless of other emotional issues, improvement in her production of /r/ through speech therapy is likely to succeed, which should alleviate the upset she has been experiencing associated with the misarticulation.

77. Three classroom management strategies:
    (1) Routines
    (2) Positive behavior support
    (3) Individualized instruction

Explanations of value:
    (1) Routines help children understand what the teacher and school expect of them every day. They also provide children with structure, which they need but usually do not know how to explain or request. Routines afford a sense of regularity and consistency; they also provide a sense of continuity from one school day to the next. For example, the teacher might instruct the children to line up every morning and wait for her to greet them. Then they go into the classroom, hang up their coats, empty their backpacks, and put their homework into a basket labeled "homework." Then they might copy that day's assignments from the board into their assignment books. When they finish that, they might work on a math or spelling game or puzzle the teacher has placed

- 107 -

on their desks. Routines should be overpracticed until the students perform them automatically. Knowing what behaviors are expected, where to find needed materials and other resources, etc., clarify and simplify children's behavioral decisions. Also, children like Alex with behavior disorders tend to find predictable, structured routines soothing.

(2) Positive behavior support systems can reduce or even end the need to punish or present negative consequences for undesirable behaviors. They do this by rewarding (reinforcing) desirable positive behaviors instead. It has been found that problem behaviors are very difficult to eradicate without identifying some more adaptive behaviors to take their place. These are called "replacement behaviors." Positive behavior support systems include routines (1). They also require classroom rules. Desirable features of classroom rules include that they are few, i.e., a total of three to six rules, with one being general; for example, "Respect yourself and respect others." Rules should also be written in positive terms and cover various situations. Positive behavior support systems can also use Positive Peer Review: students are instructed that rather than "tattle," i.e., reporting peers' bad behaviors, they should "tootle," i.e., reporting peers' good behaviors. This creates a systematic method whereby children learn to recognize positive behavior. Moreover, it enlists the entire class in supporting the positive behavior of the children with the most challenging behaviors. This in turn creates a positive classroom atmosphere and promotes positive social status for children like Alex who have emotional and/or behavioral disorders. Positive behavior support systems can also include token economy systems, lottery systems, and similar means of stimulating and reinforcing positive behaviors.

(3) Although Alex responds to others with defiance, arguing, and a negative attitude, he does want social interaction and attention from others. By giving him individualized instruction during the school day, the teacher can not only meet Alex's need for attention; she can also adapt her instruction to allow for and work around his behavior problems. The teacher can benefit from coaching, and if possible, collaboration with the psychologist or behavior specialist to incorporate techniques that are effective in his counseling sessions into academic instruction. These have not only been proven effective; adding them to classroom instruction also provides Alex with continuity between counseling and schoolwork, which will better enable him to respond consistently in changing his behavior. His teacher might even negotiate a behavioral contract with Alex, whereby he earns rewards that he values in exchange for complying with class rules and demonstrating positive behaviors.

78. Four strategies:
    (1) Review each student's IEP with the teacher
    (2) Review each student's BMP with the teacher
    (3) Model and coach differentiated instruction for the teacher
    (4) Establish procedures to stay in touch with your students

Explanations of value:
    (1) Do not assume the general education teachers will take the initiative to procure copies of all students' IEPs. Provide each teacher with a copy of the IEP for each student in your caseload; they will appreciate your saving them the time and trouble to get this information. Schedule an appointment with each teacher to review your students' IEPs. Go over each student's IEP goals and objectives with the teachers, and any differentiated instruction you have designed for meeting those goals. Find out from each teacher what

you need to supply them with that will enable them to implement this differentiated instruction, both when coteaching with you and when they are teaching alone.

(2) For those of your students who have a Behavior Management/Behavior Improvement Plan in place, go over these with the general classroom teachers. You and the classroom teachers should discuss who is responsible for implementing various portions of the plan, and which portions. You should also discuss the methods and procedures to be used; for example, behavioral contracts, point systems, reward systems, and other ways in which you will both be teaching and reinforcing the positive replacement behaviors you have identified in the behavior plan. You and the classroom teacher must have understanding and agreement about how to follow the behavior plan; if you do not, all of both your efforts will be sabotaged; the student's behavior will likely not improve; and worse, you will only end up confusing the student (which could also make the problem behaviors worse).

(3) You cannot assume that the classroom teachers will automatically know how to deliver instruction that you have designed to be differentiated for a particular student. Therefore you also cannot expect them to do so. Especially for your students who are identified with specific learning disabilities in reading, the usual instructional methods will need to be adapted. It is a good idea not only to go over these adaptations with the classroom teachers, but moreover to model for them how you apply them. One way to accomplish this if you are team-teaching is for you to teach the student initially for one or more sessions while the classroom teacher observes, and then trade roles so s/he tries your techniques while you observe. If you are teaching separately, you might arrange a few of these team sessions initially; and/or coach the classroom teacher outside of class.

(4) In middle school, you are likely to be assigned to a homeroom class. If you can arrange it, having such periods in both the morning and the afternoon will not only benefit the students and you, but will also support the classroom teachers. These twice daily periods allow you to check students' assignment books, check their homework, touch base with them about how their school day went, and keep up with any particular obstacles or challenges they may encounter during the day. These practices will help you stay in touch with the needs of your students, and any general education classroom issues with which they are currently having difficulties. You can then discuss these with the classroom teachers and work together to help the students resolve their problems.

Secret Key #1 - Time is Your Greatest Enemy

Pace Yourself

Wear a watch. At the beginning of the test, check the time (or start a chronometer on your watch to count the minutes), and check the time after every few questions to make sure you are "on schedule."

If you are forced to speed up, do it efficiently. Usually one or more answer choices can be eliminated without too much difficulty. Above all, don't panic. Don't speed up and just begin guessing at random choices. By pacing yourself, and continually monitoring your progress against your watch, you will always know exactly how far ahead or behind you are with your available time. If you find that you are one minute behind on the test, don't skip one question without spending any time on it, just to catch back up. Take 15 fewer seconds on the next four questions, and after four questions you'll have caught back up. Once you catch back up, you can continue working each problem at your normal pace.

Furthermore, don't dwell on the problems that you were rushed on. If a problem was taking up too much time and you made a hurried guess, it must be difficult. The difficult questions are the ones you are most likely to miss anyway, so it isn't a big loss. It is better to end with more time than you need than to run out of time.

Lastly, sometimes it is beneficial to slow down if you are constantly getting ahead of time. You are always more likely to catch a careless mistake by working more slowly than quickly, and among very high-scoring test takers (those who are likely to have lots of time left over), careless errors affect the score more than mastery of material.

Secret Key #2 - Guessing is not Guesswork

You probably know that guessing is a good idea. Unlike other standardized tests, there is no penalty for getting a wrong answer. Even if you have no idea about a question, you still have a 20-25% chance of getting it right.

Most test takers do not understand the impact that proper guessing can have on their score. Unless you score extremely high, guessing will significantly contribute to your final score.

Monkeys Take the Test

What most test takers don't realize is that to insure that 20-25% chance, you have to guess randomly. If you put 20 monkeys in a room to take this test, assuming they answered once per question and behaved themselves, on average they would get 20-25% of the questions correct. Put 20 test takers in the room, and the average will be much lower among guessed questions. Why?

1. The test writers intentionally write deceptive answer choices that "look" right. A test taker has no idea about a question, so he picks the "best looking" answer, which is often wrong. The monkey has no idea what looks good and what doesn't, so it will consistently be right about 20-25% of the time.
2. Test takers will eliminate answer choices from the guessing pool based on a hunch or intuition. Simple but correct answers often get excluded, leaving a 0% chance of being correct. The monkey has no clue, and often gets lucky with the best choice.

This is why the process of elimination endorsed by most test courses is flawed and detrimental to your performance. Test takers don't guess; they make an ignorant stab in the dark that is usually worse than random.

$5 Challenge

Let me introduce one of the most valuable ideas of this course—the $5 challenge:
- *You only mark your "best guess" if you are willing to bet $5 on it.*
- *You only eliminate choices from guessing if you are willing to bet $5 on it.*

Why $5? Five dollars is an amount of money that is small yet not insignificant, and can really add up fast (20 questions could cost you $100). Likewise, each answer choice on one question of the test will have a small impact on your overall score, but it can really add up to a lot of points in the end.

The process of elimination IS valuable. The following shows your chance of guessing it right:

If you eliminate wrong answer choices until only this many remain:	Chance of getting it correct:
1	100%
2	50%
3	33%

However, if you accidentally eliminate the right answer or go on a hunch for an incorrect answer, your chances drop dramatically—to 0%. By guessing among all the answer choices, you are GUARANTEED to have a shot at the right answer.

That's why the $5 test is so valuable. If you give up the advantage and safety of a pure guess, it had better be worth the risk.

What we still haven't covered is how to be sure that whatever guess you make is truly random. Here's the easiest way:
- *Always pick the first answer choice among those remaining.*

Such a technique means that you have decided, **before you see a single test question**, exactly how you are going to guess, and since the order of choices tells you nothing about which one is correct, this guessing technique is perfectly random.

This section is not meant to scare you away from making educated guesses or eliminating choices; you just need to define when a choice is worth eliminating. The $5 test, along with a pre-defined random guessing strategy, is the best way to make sure you reap all of the benefits of guessing.

Secret Key #3 - Practice Smarter, Not Harder

Many test takers delay the test preparation process because they dread the awful amounts of practice time they think necessary to succeed on the test. We have refined an effective method that will take you only a fraction of the time.

There are a number of "obstacles" in the path to success. Among these are answering questions, finishing in time, and mastering test-taking strategies. All must be executed on the day of the test at peak performance, or your score will suffer. The test is a mental marathon that has a large impact on your future.

Just like a marathon runner, it is important to work your way up to the full challenge. So first you just worry about questions, and then time, and finally strategy:

Success Strategy

1. Find a good source for practice tests.
2. If you are willing to make a larger time investment, consider using more than one study guide. Often the different approaches of multiple authors will help you "get" difficult concepts.
3. Take a practice test with no time constraints, with all study helps, "open book." Take your time with questions and focus on applying strategies.
4. Take a practice test with time constraints, with all guides, "open book."
5. Take a final practice test without open material and with time limits.

If you have time to take more practice tests, just repeat step 5. By gradually exposing yourself to the full rigors of the test environment, you will condition your mind to the stress of test day and maximize your success.

Secret Key #4 - Prepare, Don't Procrastinate

Let me state an obvious fact: if you take the test three times, you will probably get three different scores. This is due to the way you feel on test day, the level of preparedness you have, and the version of the test you see. Despite the test writers' claims to the contrary, some versions of the test WILL be easier for you than others.

Since your future depends so much on your score, you should maximize your chances of success. In order to maximize the likelihood of success, you've got to prepare in advance. This means taking practice tests and spending time learning the information and test taking strategies you will need to succeed.

Never go take the actual test as a "practice" test, expecting that you can just take it again if you need to. Take all the practice tests you can on your own, but when you go to take the official test, be prepared, be focused, and do your best the first time!

Secret Key #5 - Test Yourself

Everyone knows that time is money. There is no need to spend too much of your time or too little of your time preparing for the test. You should only spend as much of your precious time preparing as is necessary for you to get the score you need.

Once you have taken a practice test under real conditions of time constraints, then you will know if you are ready for the test or not.

If you have scored extremely high the first time that you take the practice test, then there is not much point in spending countless hours studying. You are already there.

Benchmark your abilities by retaking practice tests and seeing how much you have improved. Once you consistently score high enough to guarantee success, then you are ready.

If you have scored well below where you need, then knuckle down and begin studying in earnest. Check your improvement regularly through the use of practice tests under real conditions. Above all, don't worry, panic, or give up. The key is perseverance!

Then, when you go to take the test, remain confident and remember how well you did on the practice tests. If you can score high enough on a practice test, then you can do the same on the real thing.

General Strategies

The most important thing you can do is to ignore your fears and jump into the test immediately. Do not be overwhelmed by any strange-sounding terms. You have to jump into the test like jumping into a pool—all at once is the easiest way.

Make Predictions

As you read and understand the question, try to guess what the answer will be. Remember that several of the answer choices are wrong, and once you begin reading them, your mind will immediately become cluttered with answer choices designed to throw you off. Your mind is typically the most focused immediately after you have read the question and digested its contents. If you can, try to predict what the correct answer will be. You may be surprised at what you can predict.

Quickly scan the choices and see if your prediction is in the listed answer choices. If it is, then you can be quite confident that you have the right answer. It still won't hurt to check the other answer choices, but most of the time, you've got it!

Answer the Question

It may seem obvious to only pick answer choices that answer the question, but the test writers can create some excellent answer choices that are wrong. Don't pick an answer just because it sounds right, or you believe it to be true. It MUST answer the question. Once you've made your selection, always go back and check it against the question and make sure that you didn't misread the question and that the answer choice does answer the question posed.

Benchmark

After you read the first answer choice, decide if you think it sounds correct or not. If it doesn't, move on to the next answer choice. If it does, mentally mark that answer choice. This doesn't mean that you've definitely selected it as your answer choice, it just means that it's the best you've seen thus far. Go ahead and read the next choice. If the next choice is worse than the one you've already selected, keep going to the next answer choice. If the next choice is better than the choice you've already selected, mentally mark the new answer choice as your best guess.

The first answer choice that you select becomes your standard. Every other answer choice must be benchmarked against that standard. That choice is correct until proven otherwise by another answer choice beating it out. Once you've decided that no other answer choice seems as good, do one final check to ensure that your answer choice answers the question posed.

Valid Information

Don't discount any of the information provided in the question. Every piece of information may be necessary to determine the correct answer. None of the information in the question is there to throw you off (while the answer choices will certainly have information to throw you off). If two seemingly unrelated topics are discussed, don't ignore either. You can be confident there is a relationship, or it wouldn't be included in the question, and you are probably going to have to determine what is that relationship to find the answer.

Avoid "Fact Traps"

Don't get distracted by a choice that is factually true. Your search is for the answer that answers the question. Stay focused and don't fall for an answer that is true but irrelevant. Always go back to the question and make sure you're choosing an answer that actually answers the question and is not just a true statement. An answer can be factually correct, but it MUST answer the question asked. Additionally, two answers can both be seemingly correct, so be sure to read all of the answer choices, and make sure that you get the one that BEST answers the question.

Milk the Question

Some of the questions may throw you completely off. They might deal with a subject you have not been exposed to, or one that you haven't reviewed in years. While your lack of knowledge about the subject will be a hindrance, the question itself can give you many clues that will help you find the correct answer. Read the question carefully and look for clues. Watch particularly for adjectives and nouns describing difficult terms or words that you don't recognize. Regardless of whether you completely understand a word or not, replacing it with a synonym, either provided or one you more familiar with, may help you to understand what the questions are asking. Rather than wracking your mind about specific detailed information concerning a difficult term or word, try to use mental substitutes that are easier to understand.

The Trap of Familiarity

Don't just choose a word because you recognize it. On difficult questions, you may not recognize a number of words in the answer choices. The test writers don't put "make-believe" words on the test, so don't think that just because you only recognize all the words in one answer choice that that answer choice must be correct. If you only recognize words in one answer choice, then focus on that one. Is it correct? Try your best to determine if it is correct. If it is, that's great. If not, eliminate it. Each word and answer choice you eliminate increases your chances of getting the question correct, even if you then have to guess among the unfamiliar choices.

Eliminate Answers

Eliminate choices as soon as you realize they are wrong. But be careful! Make sure you consider all of the possible answer choices. Just because one appears right, doesn't mean that the next one won't be even better! The test writers will usually put more than one good answer choice for every question, so read all of them. Don't worry if you are stuck between two that seem right. By getting down to just two remaining possible choices, your odds are now 50/50. Rather than wasting too much time, play the odds. You are guessing, but guessing wisely because you've been able to knock out some of the answer choices that you know are wrong. If you are eliminating choices and realize that the last answer choice you are left with is also obviously wrong, don't panic. Start over and consider each choice again. There may easily be something that you missed the first time and will realize on the second pass.

Tough Questions

If you are stumped on a problem or it appears too hard or too difficult, don't waste time. Move on! Remember though, if you can quickly check for obviously incorrect answer choices, your chances of guessing correctly are greatly improved. Before you completely give up, at least try to knock out a couple of possible answers. Eliminate what you can and then guess at the remaining answer choices before moving on.

Brainstorm

If you get stuck on a difficult question, spend a few seconds quickly brainstorming. Run through the complete list of possible answer choices. Look at each choice and ask yourself, "Could this answer the question satisfactorily?" Go through each answer choice and consider it independently of the others. By systematically going through all possibilities, you may find something that you would otherwise overlook. Remember though that when you get stuck, it's important to try to keep moving.

Read Carefully

Understand the problem. Read the question and answer choices carefully. Don't miss the question because you misread the terms. You have plenty of time to read each question thoroughly and make sure you understand what is being asked. Yet a happy medium must be attained, so don't waste too much time. You must read carefully, but efficiently.

Face Value

When in doubt, use common sense. Always accept the situation in the problem at face value. Don't read too much into it. These problems will not require you to make huge leaps of logic. The test writers aren't trying to throw you off with a cheap trick. If you have to go beyond creativity and make a leap of logic in order to have an answer choice answer the question, then you should look at the other answer choices. Don't overcomplicate the problem by creating theoretical relationships or explanations that will warp time or space. These are normal problems rooted in reality. It's just that the applicable relationship or explanation may not be readily apparent and you have to figure things out. Use your common sense to interpret anything that isn't clear.

Prefixes

If you're having trouble with a word in the question or answer choices, try dissecting it. Take advantage of every clue that the word might include. Prefixes and suffixes can be a huge help. Usually they allow you to determine a basic meaning. Pre- means before, post- means after, pro - is positive, de- is negative. From these prefixes and suffixes, you can get an idea of the general meaning of the word and try to put it into context. Beware though of any traps. Just because con- is the opposite of pro-, doesn't necessarily mean congress is the opposite of progress!

Hedge Phrases

Watch out for critical hedge phrases, led off with words such as "likely," "may," "can," "sometimes," "often," "almost," "mostly," "usually," "generally," "rarely," and "sometimes." Question writers insert these hedge phrases to cover every possibility. Often an answer choice will be wrong simply because it leaves no room for exception. Unless the situation calls for them, avoid answer choices that have definitive words like "exactly," and "always."

Switchback Words

Stay alert for "switchbacks." These are the words and phrases frequently used to alert you to shifts in thought. The most common switchback word is "but." Others include "although," "however," "nevertheless," "on the other hand," "even though," "while," "in spite of," "despite," and "regardless of."

New Information

Correct answer choices will rarely have completely new information included. Answer choices typically are straightforward reflections of the material asked about and will directly relate to the question. If a new piece of information is included in an answer choice that doesn't even seem to relate to the topic being asked about, then that answer choice is likely incorrect. All of the information needed to answer the question is usually provided for you in the question. You should not have to make guesses that are unsupported or choose answer choices that require unknown information that cannot be reasoned from what is given.

Time Management

On technical questions, don't get lost on the technical terms. Don't spend too much time on any one question. If you don't know what a term means, then odds are you aren't going to get much further since you don't have a dictionary. You should be able to immediately recognize whether or not you know a term. If you don't, work with the other clues that you have—the other answer choices and terms provided—but don't waste too much time trying to figure out a difficult term that you don't know.

Contextual Clues

Look for contextual clues. An answer can be right but not the correct answer. The contextual clues will help you find the answer that is most right and is correct. Understand the context in which a phrase or statement is made. This will help you make important distinctions.

Don't Panic

Panicking will not answer any questions for you; therefore, it isn't helpful. When you first see the question, if your mind goes blank, take a deep breath. Force yourself to mechanically go through the steps of solving the problem using the strategies you've learned.

Pace Yourself

Don't get clock fever. It's easy to be overwhelmed when you're looking at a page full of questions, your mind is full of random thoughts and feeling confused, and the clock is ticking down faster than you would like. Calm down and maintain the pace that you have set for yourself. As long as you are on track by monitoring your pace, you are guaranteed to have enough time for yourself. When you get to the last few minutes of the test, it may seem like you won't have enough time left, but if you only have as many questions as you should have left at that point, then you're right on track!

Answer Selection

The best way to pick an answer choice is to eliminate all of those that are wrong, until only one is left and confirm that is the correct answer. Sometimes though, an answer choice may immediately look right. Be careful! Take a second to make sure that the other choices are not equally obvious. Don't make a hasty mistake. There are only two times that you should stop before checking other answers. First is when you are positive that the answer choice you have selected is correct. Second is when time is almost out and you have to make a quick guess!

Check Your Work

Since you will probably not know every term listed and the answer to every question, it is important that you get credit for the ones that you do know. Don't miss any questions through careless mistakes. If at all possible, try to take a second to look back over your answer selection and make sure you've selected the correct answer choice and haven't made a costly careless mistake (such as marking an answer choice that you didn't mean to mark). The time it takes for this quick double check should more than pay for itself in caught mistakes.

Beware of Directly Quoted Answers

Sometimes an answer choice will repeat word for word a portion of the question or reference section. However, beware of such exact duplication. It may be a trap! More than likely, the correct choice will paraphrase or summarize a point, rather than being exactly the same wording.

Slang

Scientific sounding answers are better than slang ones. An answer choice that begins "To compare the outcomes..." is much more likely to be correct than one that begins "Because some people insisted..."

Extreme Statements

Avoid wild answers that throw out highly controversial ideas that are proclaimed as established fact. An answer choice that states the "process should used in certain situations, if..." is much more likely to be correct than one that states the "process should be discontinued completely." The first is a calm rational statement and doesn't even make a definitive, uncompromising stance, using a hedge word "if" to provide wiggle room, whereas the second choice is a radical idea and far more extreme.

Answer Choice Families

When you have two or more answer choices that are direct opposites or parallels, one of them is usually the correct answer. For instance, if one answer choice states "x increases" and another answer choice states "x decreases" or "y increases," then those two or three answer choices are very similar in construction and fall into the same family of answer choices. A family of answer choices consists of two or three answer choices, very similar in construction, but often with directly opposite meanings. Usually the correct answer choice will be in that family of answer choices. The "odd man out" or answer choice that doesn't seem to fit the parallel construction of the other answer choices is more likely to be incorrect.

Special Report: How to Overcome Test Anxiety

The very nature of tests caters to some level of anxiety, nervousness, or tension, just as we feel for any important event that occurs in our lives. A little bit of anxiety or nervousness can be a good thing. It helps us with motivation, and makes achievement just that much sweeter. However, too much anxiety can be a problem, especially if it hinders our ability to function and perform.

"Test anxiety," is the term that refers to the emotional reactions that some test-takers experience when faced with a test or exam. Having a fear of testing and exams is based upon a rational fear, since the test-taker's performance can shape the course of an academic career. Nevertheless, experiencing excessive fear of examinations will only interfere with the test-taker's ability to perform and chance to be successful.

There are a large variety of causes that can contribute to the development and sensation of test anxiety. These include, but are not limited to, lack of preparation and worrying about issues surrounding the test.

Lack of Preparation

Lack of preparation can be identified by the following behaviors or situations:
- Not scheduling enough time to study, and therefore cramming the night before the test or exam
- Managing time poorly, to create the sensation that there is not enough time to do everything
- Failing to organize the text information in advance, so that the study material consists of the entire text and not simply the pertinent information
- Poor overall studying habits

Worrying, on the other hand, can be related to both the test taker, or many other factors around him/her that will be affected by the results of the test. These include worrying about:
- Previous performances on similar exams, or exams in general
- How friends and other students are achieving
- The negative consequences that will result from a poor grade or failure

There are three primary elements to test anxiety. Physical components, which involve the same typical bodily reactions as those to acute anxiety (to be discussed below). Emotional factors have to do with fear or panic. Mental or cognitive issues concerning attention spans and memory abilities.

Physical Signals

There are many different symptoms of test anxiety, and these are not limited to mental and emotional strain. Frequently there are a range of physical signals that will let a test taker know that he/she is suffering from test anxiety. These bodily changes can include the following:

- Perspiring
- Sweaty palms
- Wet, trembling hands
- Nausea
- Dry mouth
- A knot in the stomach
- Headache
- Faintness
- Muscle tension
- Aching shoulders, back and neck
- Rapid heart beat
- Feeling too hot/cold

To recognize the sensation of test anxiety, a test-taker should monitor him/herself for the following sensations:

- The physical distress symptoms as listed above
- Emotional sensitivity, expressing emotional feelings such as the need to cry or laugh too much, or a sensation of anger or helplessness
- A decreased ability to think, causing the test-taker to blank out or have racing thoughts that are hard to organize or control.

Though most students will feel some level of anxiety when faced with a test or exam, the majority can cope with that anxiety and maintain it at a manageable level. However, those who cannot are faced with a very real and very serious condition, which can and should be controlled for the immeasurable benefit of this sufferer.

Naturally, these sensations lead to negative results for the testing experience. The most common effects of test anxiety have to do with nervousness and mental blocking.

Nervousness

Nervousness can appear in several different levels:

- The test-taker's difficulty, or even inability to read and understand the questions on the test
- The difficulty or inability to organize thoughts to a coherent form
- The difficulty or inability to recall key words and concepts relating to the testing questions (especially essays)
- The receipt of poor grades on a test, though the test material was well known by the test taker

Conversely, a person may also experience mental blocking, which involves:

- Blanking out on test questions
- Only remembering the correct answers to the questions when the test has already finished.

Fortunately for test anxiety sufferers, beating these feelings, to a large degree, has to do with proper preparation. When a test taker has a feeling of preparedness, then anxiety will be dramatically lessened.

The first step to resolving anxiety issues is to distinguish which of the two types of anxiety are being suffered. If the anxiety is a direct result of a lack of preparation, this should be considered a normal reaction, and the anxiety level (as opposed to the test results) shouldn't be anything to worry about. However, if, when adequately prepared, the test-taker still panics, blanks out, or seems to overreact, this is not a fully rational reaction. While this can be considered normal too, there are many ways to combat and overcome these effects.

Remember that anxiety cannot be entirely eliminated, however, there are ways to minimize it, to make the anxiety easier to manage. Preparation is one of the best ways to minimize test anxiety. Therefore the following techniques are wise in order to best fight off any anxiety that may want to build.

To begin with, try to avoid cramming before a test, whenever it is possible. By trying to memorize an entire term's worth of information in one day, you'll be shocking your system, and not giving yourself a very good chance to absorb the information. This is an easy path to anxiety, so for those who suffer from test anxiety, cramming should not even be considered an option.

Instead of cramming, work throughout the semester to combine all of the material which is presented throughout the semester, and work on it gradually as the course goes by, making sure to master the main concepts first, leaving minor details for a week or so before the test.

To study for the upcoming exam, be sure to pose questions that may be on the examination, to gauge the ability to answer them by integrating the ideas from your texts, notes and lectures, as well as any supplementary readings.

If it is truly impossible to cover all of the information that was covered in that particular term, concentrate on the most important portions, that can be covered very well. Learn these concepts as best as possible, so that when the test comes, a goal can be made to use these concepts as presentations of your knowledge.

In addition to study habits, changes in attitude are critical to beating a struggle with test anxiety. In fact, an improvement of the perspective over the entire test-taking experience can actually help a test taker to enjoy studying and therefore improve the overall experience. Be certain not to overemphasize the significance of the grade - know that the result of the test is neither a reflection of self worth, nor is it a measure of intelligence; one grade will not predict a person's future success.

To improve an overall testing outlook, the following steps should be tried:

- Keeping in mind that the most reasonable expectation for taking a test is to expect to try to demonstrate as much of what you know as you possibly can.
- Reminding ourselves that a test is only one test; this is not the only one, and there will be others.
- The thought of thinking of oneself in an irrational, all-or-nothing term should be avoided at all costs.
- A reward should be designated for after the test, so there's something to look forward to. Whether it be going to a movie, going out to eat, or simply visiting friends, schedule it in advance, and do it no matter what result is expected on the exam.

Test-takers should also keep in mind that the basics are some of the most important things, even beyond anti-anxiety techniques and studying. Never neglect the basic social, emotional and biological needs, in order to try to absorb information. In order to best achieve, these three factors must be held as just as important as the studying itself.

Study Steps

Remember the following important steps for studying:
- Maintain healthy nutrition and exercise habits. Continue both your recreational activities and social pass times. These both contribute to your physical and emotional well being.
- Be certain to get a good amount of sleep, especially the night before the test, because when you're overtired you are not able to perform to the best of your best ability.
- Keep the studying pace to a moderate level by taking breaks when they are needed, and varying the work whenever possible, to keep the mind fresh instead of getting bored.
- When enough studying has been done that all the material that can be learned has been learned, and the test taker is prepared for the test, stop studying and do something relaxing such as listening to music, watching a movie, or taking a warm bubble bath.

There are also many other techniques to minimize the uneasiness or apprehension that is experienced along with test anxiety before, during, or even after the examination. In fact, there are a great deal of things that can be done to stop anxiety from interfering with lifestyle and performance. Again, remember that anxiety will not be eliminated entirely, and it shouldn't be. Otherwise that "up" feeling for exams would not exist, and most of us depend on that sensation to perform better than usual. However, this anxiety has to be at a level that is manageable.

Of course, as we have just discussed, being prepared for the exam is half the battle right away. Attending all classes, finding out what knowledge will be expected on the exam, and knowing the exam schedules are easy steps to lowering anxiety. Keeping up with work will remove the need to cram, and efficient study habits will eliminate wasted time. Studying should be done in an ideal location for concentration, so that it is simple to become interested in the material and give it complete attention. A method such as SQ3R (Survey, Question, Read, Recite, Review) is a wonderful key to follow to make sure that the study habits are as effective as possible, especially in the case of learning from a textbook. Flashcards are great techniques for memorization. Learning to take good notes will mean that notes will be full of useful information, so that less sifting will need to be done to seek out what is pertinent for studying. Reviewing notes after class and then again on occasion will keep the information fresh in the mind. From notes that have been taken summary sheets and outlines can be made for simpler reviewing.

A study group can also be a very motivational and helpful place to study, as there will be a sharing of ideas, all of the minds can work together, to make sure that everyone understands, and the studying will be made more interesting because it will be a social occasion.

Basically, though, as long as the test-taker remains organized and self confident, with efficient study habits, less time will need to be spent studying, and higher grades will be achieved.

To become self confident, there are many useful steps. The first of these is "self talk." It has been shown through extensive research, that self-talk for students who suffer from test anxiety, should be well monitored, in order to make sure that it contributes to self confidence as opposed to sinking the student. Frequently the self talk of test-anxious students is negative or self-defeating, thinking that everyone else is smarter and faster, that they always mess up, and that if they don't do well, they'll fail the entire course. It is important to decreasing anxiety that awareness is made of self talk. Try writing any negative self thoughts and then disputing them with a positive statement instead. Begin self-encouragement as though it was a friend speaking. Repeat positive statements to help reprogram the mind to believing in successes instead of failures.

Helpful Techniques

Other extremely helpful techniques include:
- Self-visualization of doing well and reaching goals
- While aiming for an "A" level of understanding, don't try to "overprotect" by setting your expectations lower. This will only convince the mind to stop studying in order to meet the lower expectations.
- Don't make comparisons with the results or habits of other students. These are individual factors, and different things work for different people, causing different results.
- Strive to become an expert in learning what works well, and what can be done in order to improve. Consider collecting this data in a journal.
- Create rewards for after studying instead of doing things before studying that will only turn into avoidance behaviors.
- Make a practice of relaxing - by using methods such as progressive relaxation, self-hypnosis, guided imagery, etc - in order to make relaxation an automatic sensation.
- Work on creating a state of relaxed concentration so that concentrating will take on the focus of the mind, so that none will be wasted on worrying.
- Take good care of the physical self by eating well and getting enough sleep.
- Plan in time for exercise and stick to this plan.

Beyond these techniques, there are other methods to be used before, during and after the test that will help the test-taker perform well in addition to overcoming anxiety.

Before the exam comes the academic preparation. This involves establishing a study schedule and beginning at least one week before the actual date of the test. By doing this, the anxiety of not having enough time to study for the test will be automatically eliminated. Moreover, this will make the studying a much more effective experience, ensuring that the learning will be an easier process. This relieves much undue pressure on the test-taker.

Summary sheets, note cards, and flash cards with the main concepts and examples of these main concepts should be prepared in advance of the actual studying time. A topic should never be eliminated from this process. By omitting a topic because it isn't expected to be on the test is only setting up the test-taker for anxiety should it actually appear on the exam. Utilize the course syllabus for laying out the topics that should be studied. Carefully go over the notes that were made in class, paying special attention to any of the issues that the professor took special care to emphasize while lecturing in class. In the textbooks, use the chapter review, or if possible, the chapter tests, to begin your review.

It may even be possible to ask the instructor what information will be covered on the exam, or what the format of the exam will be (for example, multiple choice, essay, free form, true-false). Additionally, see if it is possible to find out how many questions will be on the test. If a review sheet or sample test has been offered by the professor, make good use of it, above anything else, for the preparation for the test. Another great resource for getting to know the examination is reviewing tests from previous semesters. Use these tests to review, and aim to achieve a 100% score on each of the possible topics. With a few exceptions, the goal that you set for yourself is the highest one that you will reach.

Take all of the questions that were assigned as homework, and rework them to any other possible course material. The more problems reworked, the more skill and confidence will form as a result. When forming the solution to a problem, write out each of the steps. Don't simply do head work. By doing as many steps on paper as possible, much clarification and therefore confidence will be formed. Do this with as many homework problems as possible, before checking the answers. By checking the answer after each problem, a reinforcement will exist, that will not be on the exam. Study situations should be as exam-like as possible, to prime the test-taker's system for the experience. By waiting to check the answers at the end, a psychological advantage will be formed, to decrease the stress factor.

Another fantastic reason for not cramming is the avoidance of confusion in concepts, especially when it comes to mathematics. 8-10 hours of study will become one hundred percent more effective if it is spread out over a week or at least several days, instead of doing it all in one sitting. Recognize that the human brain requires time in order to assimilate new material, so frequent breaks and a span of study time over several days will be much more beneficial.

Additionally, don't study right up until the point of the exam. Studying should stop a minimum of one hour before the exam begins. This allows the brain to rest and put things in their proper order. This will also provide the time to become as relaxed as possible when going into the examination room. The test-taker will also have time to eat well and eat sensibly. Know that the brain needs food as much as the rest of the body. With enough food and enough sleep, as well as a relaxed attitude, the body and the mind are primed for success.

Avoid any anxious classmates who are talking about the exam. These students only spread anxiety, and are not worth sharing the anxious sentimentalities.

Before the test also involves creating a positive attitude, so mental preparation should also be a point of concentration. There are many keys to creating a positive attitude. Should fears become rushing in, make a visualization of taking the exam, doing well, and seeing an A written on the paper. Write out a list of affirmations that will bring a feeling of confidence, such as "I am doing well in my English class," "I studied well and know my material," "I enjoy this class." Even if the affirmations aren't believed at first, it sends a positive message to the subconscious which will result in an alteration of the overall belief system, which is the system that creates reality.

If a sensation of panic begins, work with the fear and imagine the very worst! Work through the entire scenario of not passing the test, failing the entire course, and dropping out of school, followed by not getting a job, and pushing a shopping cart through the dark alley where you'll live. This will place things into perspective! Then, practice deep breathing and create a visualization of the opposite situation - achieving an "A" on the exam, passing the entire course, receiving the degree at a graduation ceremony.

On the day of the test, there are many things to be done to ensure the best results, as well as the most calm outlook. The following stages are suggested in order to maximize test-taking potential:

- Begin the examination day with a moderate breakfast, and avoid any coffee or beverages with caffeine if the test taker is prone to jitters. Even people who are used to managing caffeine can feel jittery or light-headed when it is taken on a test day.
- Attempt to do something that is relaxing before the examination begins. As last minute cramming clouds the mastering of overall concepts, it is better to use this time to create a calming outlook.
- Be certain to arrive at the test location well in advance, in order to provide time to select a location that is away from doors, windows and other distractions, as well as giving enough time to relax before the test begins.
- Keep away from anxiety generating classmates who will upset the sensation of stability and relaxation that is being attempted before the exam.
- Should the waiting period before the exam begins cause anxiety, create a self-distraction by reading a light magazine or something else that is relaxing and simple.

During the exam itself, read the entire exam from beginning to end, and find out how much time should be allotted to each individual problem. Once writing the exam, should more time be taken for a problem, it should be abandoned, in order to begin another problem. If there is time at the end, the unfinished problem can always be returned to and completed.

Read the instructions very carefully - twice - so that unpleasant surprises won't follow during or after the exam has ended.

When writing the exam, pretend that the situation is actually simply the completion of homework within a library, or at home. This will assist in forming a relaxed atmosphere, and will allow the brain extra focus for the complex thinking function.

Begin the exam with all of the questions with which the most confidence is felt. This will build the confidence level regarding the entire exam and will begin a quality momentum. This will also create encouragement for trying the problems where uncertainty resides.

Going with the "gut instinct" is always the way to go when solving a problem. Second guessing should be avoided at all costs. Have confidence in the ability to do well.

For essay questions, create an outline in advance that will keep the mind organized and make certain that all of the points are remembered. For multiple choice, read every answer, even if the correct one has been spotted - a better one may exist.

Continue at a pace that is reasonable and not rushed, in order to be able to work carefully. Provide enough time to go over the answers at the end, to check for small errors that can be corrected.

Should a feeling of panic begin, breathe deeply, and think of the feeling of the body releasing sand through its pores. Visualize a calm, peaceful place, and include all of the sights, sounds and sensations of this image. Continue the deep breathing, and take a few minutes to continue this with closed eyes. When all is well again, return to the test.

If a "blanking" occurs for a certain question, skip it and move on to the next question. There will be time to return to the other question later. Get everything done that can be done, first, to guarantee all the grades that can be compiled, and to build all of the confidence possible. Then return to the weaker questions to build the marks from there.

Remember, one's own reality can be created, so as long as the belief is there, success will follow. And remember: anxiety can happen later, right now, there's an exam to be written!

After the examination is complete, whether there is a feeling for a good grade or a bad grade, don't dwell on the exam, and be certain to follow through on the reward that was promised...and enjoy it! Don't dwell on any mistakes that have been made, as there is nothing that can be done at this point anyway.

Additionally, don't begin to study for the next test right away. Do something relaxing for a while, and let the mind relax and prepare itself to begin absorbing information again.

From the results of the exam - both the grade and the entire experience, be certain to learn from what has gone on. Perfect studying habits and work some more on confidence in order to make the next examination experience even better than the last one.

Learn to avoid places where openings occurred for laziness, procrastination and day dreaming.

Use the time between this exam and the next one to better learn to relax, even learning to relax on cue, so that any anxiety can be controlled during the next exam. Learn how to relax the body. Slouch in your chair if that helps. Tighten and then relax all of the different muscle groups, one group at a time, beginning with the feet and then working all the way up to the neck and face. This will ultimately relax the muscles more than they were to begin with. Learn how to breathe deeply and comfortably, and focus on this breathing going in and out as a relaxing thought. With every exhale, repeat the word "relax."

As common as test anxiety is, it is very possible to overcome it. Make yourself one of the test-takers who overcome this frustrating hindrance.

Additional Bonus Material

Due to our efforts to try to keep this book to a manageable length, we've created a link that will give you access to all of your additional bonus material.

Please visit http://www.mometrix.com/bonus948/megammccsped to access the information.